Competition in lending and credit ratings

Javed I. Ahmed*

April 16, 2014

Abstract

This article relates corporate credit rating quality to competition in lending between the public bond market and banks. In the model, the monopolistic rating agency's choice of price and quality leads to an endogenous threshold separating low-quality bank-dependent issuers from higher-quality issuers with access to public debt. In a baseline equilibrium with expensive bank lending, this separation across debt market segments provides information, but equilibrium ratings are uninformative. A positive shock to private (bank) relative to public lending supply allows banks to compete with public lenders for high-quality issuers, which threatens rating agency profits, and informative ratings result to prevent defection of high-quality borrowers to banks. This prediction is tested by analyzing two events that increased the relative supply of private vs. public lending sharply: legislation in 1994 that reduced barriers to interstate bank lending and the temporary shutdown of the high-yield bond market in 1989. After each event, the quality of ratings (based on their impact on bond yield spreads) increased for affected issuers. The analysis suggests that that the quality of credit ratings plays an important role in financial stability, as strategic behavior by the rating agency in an issuer-pays setting dampens the influence of macroeconomic shocks. It also explains the use of informative unsolicited credit ratings to prevent unrated bond issues, particularly during good times. Additionally, the controversial issuer-pays model of ratings leads to more efficient outcomes than investor-pays alternatives.

1 Introduction

While the importance of credit ratings for access to public debt markets is widely accepted, incentives to produce high-quality ratings remain controversial. Some expect ratings to be informative, citing the agencies' stated objectives. Others suggest the issuer-pays business model might lead to bias and ratings shopping (which some investors cannot perceive), or that accuracy in the short term may allow a rating agency to fool investors later. Relative to such alternatives, the role of competition in lending across debt market segments has received limited consideration.

This paper analyzes the debt issuer's decision to purchase a rating from a strategic rating agency and seek investment from banks or public markets. The model suggests a previously-overlooked competitive channel (between banks and bond investors) influences incentives to accurately reveal information in ratings. Analysis of shocks to relative lending supply allows identification in tests of the model's prediction that increased competition from banks leads to more informative credit ratings for corporate issuers.

In the model, a monopolistic rating agency sets the price and quality of credit ratings. Arms-length public investors know only the issuer's rating, while private lenders can learn the issuer's quality but require a higher return.[1] The rating agency's action trades off low-quality issuers' desire to pool against the threat that high-quality issuers may borrow from private lenders (banks) if ratings do not allow them to separate. High-quality customers' defection affects the rating agency directly through lost revenue from these customers, and indirectly by reducing the value of ratings for all customers. This externality operates through beliefs about rated issuer quality, and links the informativeness of credit ratings to the threat posed by banks.

Identification of the influence of private lenders on rating informativeness is complicated

---

[1]This higher return could arise because private lenders incur monitoring costs or have a lower discount rate, or it could represent the borrower's preference for dealing with arms-length public investors.

by difficulties in separately identifying supply and demand, and by challenges specific to measuring total private lending. Studies by Faulkender and Petersen (2006) and Leary (2009) suggest that shifts in loan supply affect the firm's choice between public and private borrowing. An ideal test of the influence of competition relates this borrowing choice directly to the rating agency's informativeness decision.

To test how competition from private lenders influences ratings informativeness, I identify and analyze two events which increased the relative supply of private vs. public lending. The first event I analyze is the Riegle-Neal Interstate Banking and Branching Efficiency Act of 1994 (the "Riegle-Neal Act"). This legislation reduced barriers to interstate branching (Dick, 2006), and had a disproportional affect for young issuers, since older issuers had access to interstate borrowing before the legislation (Zarutskie, 2006). By increasing the supply of private lending for young issuers, without having a similar impact on the supply of public lending, this legislation shifted the relative supply of private vs. public lending for young issuers.

I also examine the 1989 collapse of Drexel Burnham Lambert (the "Drexel collapse"), which led to the temporary shutdown of the high-yield bond market. Lemmon and Roberts (2010) argue that this collapse was exogenous with respect to demand for borrowing. Because it was concentrated in the high-yield segment of the public debt market, I argue that it increased the relative supply of private vs. public lending for high-yield issuers more than it did for investment-grade issuers.

I analyze how each event affected the informativeness of ratings by comparing issuers facing differential shifts to the relative supply of private vs. public lending. I measure informativeness based on the estimated coefficient on the credit rating from a regression of the yield spread for a new issue on the rating and a set of issue- and issuer-level control variables. This measure of informativeness is based on the premise that when ratings contain information relative to what investors know, investors pay more for a bond issue that

2

is rated higher than expected. By contrast, uninformative ratings have a lower impact on bond pricing. I find that rating informativeness increased significantly following both the Drexel collapse and the Riegle-Neal Act for a subset of affected issuers, compared with a control group not impacted by the supply shifts. These results suggest that the quality of ratings responds to competition between private and public lenders.

My model also offers an explanation for the controversial practice of issuing unsolicited credit ratings.[2] It suggests such ratings should be informative. In the model, the rating agency's choice of ratings informativeness and the rating fee lead to an endogenous threshold quality level, such that all issuers with higher quality purchase ratings. By raising the average quality of unrated firms, increases in this threshold present the possibility that unrated issuers can access public markets. Such access jeopardizes the gatekeeper status of the rating agency, and reduces fees it can charge for solicited ratings. Unsolicited ratings act as a strategic pricing tool that allows the rating agency to extract higher rents from paying customers. However, unsolicited ratings lead to underinvestment when borrowers with positive-NPV projects that do not receive unsolicited ratings are unable to raise financing.

The rest of this paper is organized as follows. The next two sections discuss related literature and institutional background. Section 4 introduces the model, analyzes equilibrium outcomes and discusses implications for efficiency. Section 5 discusses methodology and section 6 presents empirical results. Section 7 concludes. I present proofs in Appendix A.

---

[2]Standard & Poor's has an explicit policy to rate all significant corporate bond issues, whether or not the issuer pays (Cantor and Packer, 1994).

2 Related literature

This paper is related to the literature on ratings determination and standards, ratings informativeness, and rating agency incentives. It adds to the rating informativeness literature by exploring whether information in ratings is new relative to fundamentals. By relating informative ratings to competition from private lenders, my paper suggests a new competitive channel is important for rating agency incentives.

Lizzeri (1999) considers the rating agency's incentive to make ratings informative, and suggests that low-quality marginal customers prefer uninformative ratings, while high-quality rating customers are captive. In his model, the rating agency caters to low-quality customers with ratings that distinguish between rated and unrated issuers, but do not contain additional information. This result is compelling, but contrasts with both intuition and evidence that suggests ratings are informative (e.g., Kliger and Sarig, 2000; Jorion, Liu and Shi, 2005).

Related studies that analyze ratings determination (e.g., Horrigan, 1966; Kaplan and Urwitz, 1979; Ederington, 1985; Kraft, 2011) focus on the relationship between observable firm characteristics and credit ratings. Studies of rating standards (e.g., Amato and Furfine, 2004; Blume, Lim, and MacKinlay, 2006) focus on variation in the relationship between ratings and fundamentals over time. A number of studies address the informativeness of ratings, usually by analyzing the stock or bond price reaction to upgrades and downgrades.[3]

To relate the informativeness of ratings to rating agency incentives, I focus on ratings assigned to new issues, which comprise the majority of rating fees for corporate issuers (White, 2001). My approach for measuring ratings informativeness is closest to that of Liu and Thakor (1984) and Becker and Milbourn (2011) who consider the effect of ratings on bond yields. This approach measures the incremental impact of ratings (above fundamentals) by regressing bond yields on credit ratings, using control variables that predict the rating.

---

[3]Examples include Holthausen and Leftwich (1986), Hand, Holthausen, and Leftwich (1992), Kliger and Sarig (2000), Dichev and Piotroski (2001), Hull, Predescu, and White (2004), and Jorion, Liu, and Shi (2005).

Several recent studies on rating agency incentives suggest that reputation-building (by rating agencies), competition between rating agencies, and regulatory distortions influence the information content of ratings. Reputation-based studies (Mathis, MacAndrews, and Rochet, 2009; Bolton, Freixas and Shapiro, 2012; and Bar-Isaac and Shapiro, 2012) argue that when there are more issuances (for example, during boom times), accuracy declines because building reputation becomes less important. These results depend on the value of reputation, which in turn depends on the rating agency's discount rate (and, possibly, on investors' ability to understand rating agency incentives). A truth-telling equilibrium arises in these models when the value of reputation is sufficiently high.

Studies of regulatory distortions and competition between rating agencies suggest both factors lead to less informative ratings. This could be due to regulatory arbitrage (Opp, Opp, and Harris, 2013) or ratings shopping (Skreta and Veldkamp, 2009). Doherty, Kartasheva, and Phillips (2012) suggest informative ratings may prevent entry in the ratings sector. Becker and Milbourn (2011) analyze the effects of competition using Fitch's market share and find ratings are less informative when Fitch's market share is higher. I argue that competition between public and private lenders plays an important role, and that competition between agencies in the corporate bond rating sector has been relatively limited.

We have few explanations for the rating agency's incentives to issue unsolicited ratings. Sangiorgi, Sokobin and Spatt (2009) suggest that such ratings allow agencies to avoid litigation. Fulghieri, Strobl, and Xia (2013) suggest downward-biased unsolicited ratings force issuers to pay higher fees for solicited ratings. Unsolicited ratings are also lower than solicited ratings in my model, but are not biased, and must be informative even if based on public information. Smaller rating agencies argue such ratings are anti-competitive; my paper also relates unsolicited ratings to market power, but suggests they may emerge without threat of entry into the ratings sector.

This paper is the first, to my knowledge, to explicitly focus on how strategic actions of credit rating agencies affect the public debt issuance threshold. The main difference between my model and standard information intermediary models (Lizzeri, 1999; Faure-Grimaud, Peyrache, and Quesada, 2009) is that I model debt issuers rather than asset sales. Lizzeri's (1999) sellers have the same value for a given rating. By contrast, payoffs for debt issuers in my model depend on issuer quality, even conditional on the rating. This dependence leads to possible underinvestment: outcomes in which some borrowers do not pursue their positive-NPV projects.

Finally, this paper relates broadly to literature that analyzes the choice between private and public debt. In contrast to classic studies that explicitly model the role of private lenders (e.g. Sharpe, 1990; Diamond, 1991; Rajan, 1992), my paper treats the cost of private borrowing as exogenous. In my model, the rating agency, acting on behalf of public lenders, uses informative ratings to compete with private lenders. My results suggest that arms-length public lenders are not passive players in debt markets, and instead compete actively using the ratings sector.

3 Institutional background

I briefly summarize some institutional features of the credit ratings industry that motivate this analysis. Bond rating agencies were established during the early 20th century, primarily in response to asymmetric information problems related to investments in U.S. railroad corporations, and gained prominence through inclusion in regulation during the post-depression era. [4] Today, there are three major players in the corporate credit rating market: Standard & Poor's ("S&P", a unit of the McGraw Hill Companies), Moodys Corporation ("Moodys"), and Fitch Ratings ("Fitch").

---

[4]See Sylla, 2001, for a discussion of the origins of the industry or Cantor and Packer, 1994, for a summary of relevant regulation.

Regulatory and voluntary constraints on institutional investment lead to rating-based segmentation of bond investors. Regulation in 1931 increased the importance of rating agencies, and required banks to mark low-rated securities to market (Cantor and Packer, 1994). In 1936, regulation prohibited banks from purchasing "speculative" securities, where the definition of "speculative" was based on credit ratings from at least two major agencies (Sylla, 2001). In 1975, the Securities and Exchange Commission initiated the Nationally Recognized Statistical Rating Agency ("NRSRO") distinction, which defined the set of ratings entities whose ratings could be used for regulatory purposes (White, 2001). Subsequent regulation imposed rating-based formulae into determination of capital and margin lending requirements, often granting favorable treatment to highly-rated (AAA) bonds (Cantor and Packer, 1994).

Public markets for corporate bonds remain segmented across two important boundaries: the "investment-grade boundary," and the "high-grade boundary," with the latter emphasizing AAA-rated issuers. Segmented markets pose empirical challenges for empirical studies that analyze the effects of particular credit ratings. When measuring ratings numerically, one rating category is more important when the rating change involved causes the issuer to cross the high-grade or investment-grade boundary. Additionally, while not an explicit requirement for raising public debt, first-time issues of public debt are almost always rated, and the potential for raising public debt without a rating is limited.

The rating agencies business model includes charging the issuer of securities, rather than investors. This "issuer pays" model has been the subject of controversy, as several studies have suggested this could lead to conflicts of interest and overly customer-friendly ratings (Skreta and Veldkamp, 2010). Such studies typically require an assumption about investors inability to recognize the conflicts in the issuer-pays model. This article suggests a countervailing benefit of the issuer pays model: rating fees may allow bond issuers to signal their quality (and lead otherwise-marginal issuers to choose a safe project which does not require financing).

The ability of firms to shop for ratings and engage in regulatory arbitrage depends on the number of possible rating agencies and on whether these agencies' ratings are viewed as substitutes. Here, the structured finance and corporate bond markets served by the rating agencies differ. While several studies (for example, Skreta and Veldkamp, 2010, Mathis, MacAndrews and Rochet, 2010, or Benmelech and Dlugosz, 2010) have ascribed deterioration in credit rating quality to ratings shopping, such studies have focused on the structured finance market. Additionally, studies that analyze "issuer-friendly" ratings and rating agency capture (through ratings that are biased upwards) rely on an assumption about limited investor rationality (since rational investors discount the rating they expect to be biased).

By contrast, competition in the corporate bond rating market has been limited. The three major players have over 90% market share, with Fitch lagging far behind Moodys and S&P (Becker and Milbourn, 2010). Nearly all bond issues in studies by Bongaerts, Cremers and Goetzman (2010) have ratings from S&P and Moodys, and many also have ratings from Fitch. The only variable in terms of issuer behavior in the corporate bond market appears to be whether to purchase a rating from Fitch: ratings from S&P and Moodys are purchased for nearly all rated new issues. This suggests these two agencies enjoy an oligopoly, and distortions from ratings shopping are less significant in corporate bond markets than in markets for structured finance.

4 Model

Consider a one-period economy with risk-neutral agents in which a firm's owner-operator ("he", or the "entrepreneur") chooses whether to raise financing to invest in a risky project from either public or private lenders. The entrepreneur has (fungible) initial assets A, and his quality $\theta \sim U[0, 1]$ represents his privately-known probability of success with the risky project. The risky project requires capital $K > A$, and produces cash flow X if successful (otherwise, it produces 0).

The entrepreneur has three investment alternatives. He can deploy his assets in a risk free project which returns zero, borrow from public lenders, or borrow from private lenders. Private lenders can learn θ, but require expected return $P > 0$ in order to lend, while competitive public-market investors need only break even (earn zero expected return). $P > 0$ captures the assumption that public borrowing is less costly from the perspective of the issuer than private borrowing. This can be because of monitoring costs, differences in discount rates, or because the issuer prefers to deal with arms-length investors.

The rating agency offers to produce rating $r \in [0, 1]$ with informativeness α in exchange for fee ϕ, and can credibly commit to a rating disclosure policy. I restrict consideration to full disclosure by the rating agency,[5] and allow it to choose (without cost) the probability (α) with which it observes and discloses θ. The informativeness of the rating represents the probability with which it reveals the type of the entrepreneur. With probability α, the rating reveals his quality: $r = \theta$. With probability $(1 - \alpha)$, the rating is not revealing, and investors know only that the issuer purchased a rating. As discussed below, this is equivalent to setting investor beliefs equal to the average quality of rated issuers: $r = E[\theta \mid \text{issuer rated}]$. I initially assume the rating agency cannot issue unsolicited ratings; I relax this assumption in Section 4.2.

This signal structure emphasizes the role of ratings informativeness on the entrepreneur's ex ante decision to purchase a rating. Investors know whether the rating they observe is informative.[6] To understand this signal structure, consider an uninformative rating scheme:

---

[5]I assume truth-telling can be enforced because the value of reputation is sufficiently high. This is a possible equilibrium outcome in Mathis et al. (2009) and Bolton et al. (2010).

[6]In practice, investors are likely unable to distinguish directly between informative and uninformative ratings. The signal structure I use captures the idea that when ratings are informative, investors place more weight on ratings in estimating issuer quality.

$\alpha = 0$. If such a rating is costly ($\phi > 0$), it allows the entrepreneur to signal because low-quality entrepreneurs will prefer investing in the safe project to purchasing a rating. In this way, α captures informativeness of ratings beyond information in the rating purchase decision.

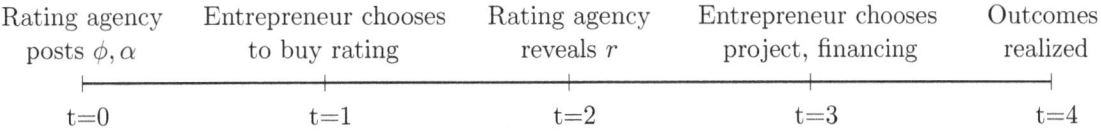

Rating agency posts ϕ, α	Entrepreneur chooses to buy rating	Rating agency reveals r	Entrepreneur chooses project, financing	Outcomes realized
t=0	t=1	t=2	t=3	t=4

Figure 1: Timing of moves

The timing of events is summarized in Figure 1. At $t = 0$, the rating agency chooses the rating fee, ϕ, and rating informativeness, α. At $t = 1$, the entrepreneur decides whether to obtain a rating. The rating is produced and disclosed at $t = 2$, and investors update beliefs about the entrepreneur's quality. Next, at $t = 3$, the entrepreneur decides whether to invest in the safe project or the risky project, using required repayment levels implied by investors' beliefs to evaluate expected $t = 4$ payoffs. If the entrepreneur chooses the risky project, he raises financing by offering repayment $R \in \{R(r), R^{\mathrm{U}}, R^{\mathrm{P}}\}$ which depends on whether he seeks public financing with rating r, is unrated, or seeks private financing. At $t = 4$, project outcomes and payoffs are realized.

4.1 Equilibrium with informative ratings

I consider symmetric Bayesian-Nash equilibria of the game. An equilibrium $\{\phi, \alpha, \Theta\}$ consists of a fee, rating informativeness, and a set of decision rules for each type of entrepreneur. I solve the model by backwards induction. At $t = 3$, the entrepreneur decides whether to raise financing and the financing type. I first rule out financing when entrepreneurs invest less than A.

Lemma 1: *There is no equilibrium in which an entrepreneur invests less than A in the risky*

10

project.

Lemma 1 suggests that all entrepreneurs must invest their assets in the risky project (because not doing so would be a negative signal). The amount of financing is $K + \phi - A$ if the entrepreneur purchases a rating, and $K - A$ otherwise.[7] At $t = 4$, investors are repaid if the project is successful. If it is not, the investors and entrepreneur receive 0. Because there are no funds to repay debt if the project is unsuccessful, required repayment refers to the amount promised to investors if the project succeeds. If the entrepreneur raises public financing, promised repayment at $t = 3$ depends on the $t = 2$ rating and satisfies investors' participation conditions: public investors expect to break even, while private investors require expected return P. At $t = 1$, the entrepreneur chooses whether to purchase a rating. At $t = 0$, the rating agency chooses ϕ and α to maximize profits.

For high-quality entrepreneurs, informative ratings are favorable and uninformative ratings are unfavorable, while the reverse is true for low-quality entrepreneurs. For high-quality entrepreneurs, an unfavorable (uninformative) rating may lead to a preference for bank financing, while for low-quality entrepreneurs, an unfavorable (informative) rating may lead to preference for the safe project. If the rating is informative, investors know the entrepreneur has quality θ, while if it is uninformative they believe the entrepreneur's quality is equal to the average quality of rated entrepreneurs.

Because the entrepreneur's profit is increasing in θ, I solve for an equilibrium in which there exist quality thresholds that define the strategy of each type of entrepreneur. Because private lenders learn the entrepreneur's quality, high-quality entrepreneurs benefit more from private borrowing. Because they value the risky project less, low-quality entrepreneurs are more likely to choose the safe project. I assume that the entrepreneur first pays for the rating, then makes an investment decision conditional on the rating outcome. A consequence

---

[7]The assumption that the owner-manager of the issuing firm cannot invest outside wealth in the project shuts off the signaling mechanism of Leland and Pyle (1977).

is that some low-quality entrepreneurs purchase a rating, hoping it will be uninformative so they can pool with high-quality entrepreneurs. Similarly, some high quality entrepreneurs purchase a rating, hoping it will be informative and allow them to separate from low-quality entrepreneurs.

To seek financing, the entrepreneur must expect to earn more than A, which could be obtained by investing in the safe project:

$$\theta(X - R) \geq A \tag{1}$$

where R, the amount promised to investors if the project succeeds, depends on the rating only if the entrepreneur seeks public borrowing. Each type of financing satisfies investors' break-even conditions: public market lenders are competitive, while private lenders require return P. Repayment for rated entrepreneurs is:

$$R(r) = \frac{K - A + \phi}{E[\theta|\, r]} \tag{2}$$

while private borrowing requires repayment:

$$R^{\mathrm{P}} = \frac{K - A + P}{\theta}. \tag{3}$$

Repayment for unrated entrepreneurs public borrowers is:

$$R^{\mathrm{U}} = \frac{K - A}{E[\theta|\mathrm{unrated}]}, \tag{4}$$

which yields expected profits for unrated public issuers:

$$\theta \left[X - \left(\frac{K - A}{E[\theta|\, \mathrm{unrated}]} \right) \right]. \tag{5}$$

To decide whether to get rated, the entrepreneur calculates payoffs conditional on having a rating. After paying the fee, the entrepreneur will receive either an informative or uninformative rating, with which it can seek public financing. Its expected $t = 4$ payoff

12

under each alternative is:

$$\theta X - K + A - \phi \quad \text{public financing with informative rating} \qquad (6)$$

$$\theta\left[X - \left(\frac{(K - A + \phi)}{E[\theta \mid \text{rated }]}\right)\right] \quad \text{public borrowing with uninformative rating} \qquad (7)$$

$$\theta X - K + A - P - \phi \quad \text{rated, but chooses private borrowing} \qquad (8)$$

$$A - \phi \quad \text{rated, but chooses the safe project} \qquad (9)$$

Having paid the fee, the entrepreneur may decide to seek private financing or to invest in the safe project. The entrepreneur raises public financing when doing so (with rating r) is preferable to both the safe project and private borrowing:

$$\theta[X - R(r)] \geq \text{Max}\Big(\underbrace{A - \phi}_{\text{safe project}} , \quad \underbrace{\theta X - (K - A + P + \phi)}_{\text{private borrowing}} \Big) \qquad (10)$$

While ϕ in Equation (10) is a sunk cost from the perspective of the entrepreneur, it still influences the value of alternatives to public lending. The entrepreneur accounts for the possibility that he may not like the rating outcome. If he decides not to seek public financing after purchasing the rating, he will have less to invest in the safe project, and must borrow more from private lenders to invest in the risky project.

Before defining the strategy for each type of entrepreneur, I examine some implications of Equations (1) - (10). Consider a rated entrepreneur who prefers private borrowing to raising public financing. By examining Equation (10), which assumes a rating has already been purchased, we see that high-quality entrepreneurs prefer private borrowing, while low-quality entrepreneurs prefer the safe project. These preferences are maintained as θ increases: if an entrepreneur prefers private borrowing to public borrowing, or public borrowing to the safe project, higher-quality entrepreneurs share these preferences.

This suggests entrepreneurs who prefer public financing to purchasing a rating are high-quality entrepreneurs, while those who prefer the safe project to public financing have lower quality. Next, consider the entrepreneur's ability to borrow from public lenders without

13

a rating. Such an entrepreneur is likely to have higher quality than an entrepreneur who prefers the safe project, because choosing the risky project links payoffs to quality. However, he is unwilling to pay the rating fee, suggesting his quality is lower than that of a rated entrepreneur.

Thus, it is natural to define entrepreneur strategies using quality thresholds. I summarize the strategy of each type of entrepreneur using thresholds $\Theta \equiv \{\theta_U, \theta_L, \theta_{LU}, \theta_{HU}, \theta_H\}$ such that entrepreneurs with quality $\theta < \theta_U$ choose the safe project, $\theta \in [\theta_U, \theta_L)$ pursue public financing without a rating, $\theta \in [\theta_L, \theta_{LU})$ raise public financing conditional on the rating outcome (and choose the safe project if the rating is not favorable), $\theta \in [\theta_{LU}, \theta_{HU})$ purchase a rating and raise public financing unconditionally, $\theta \in [\theta_{HU}, \theta_H)$ purchase a rating but raise public financing conditional on the rating (and choose private financing if the rating is not favorable), and $\theta \in (\theta_H, 1]$ choose private financing. If $\theta_L > \theta_{LU}$, all rated entrepreneurs prefer public financing to the safe project regardless of the rating. The set of thresholds is illustrated in Figure 2.

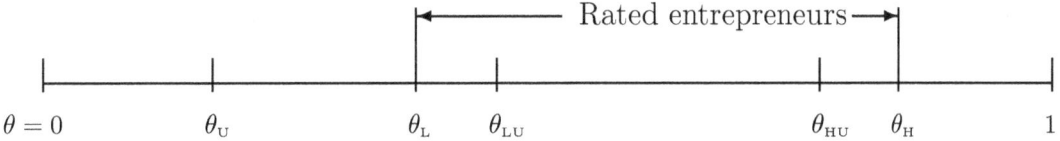

Figure 2: Entrepreneur quality notation.

This figure illustrates the notation used for entrepreneur decision thresholds. Entrepreneur quality represents the probability the entrepreneur's risky project will succeed. Entrepreneurs with quality $\theta \in [\theta_L, \theta_H]$ purchase ratings, and a subset of these entrepreneurs with quality $\theta \in [\theta_{LU}, \theta_{HU}]$ raises public financing regardless of the rating outcome. The average rated entrepreneur has quality $(\theta_H + \theta_L)/2$. θ_U is the threshold for raising public financing without a rating.

For each threshold, I verify that no entrepreneur can profitably deviate, and then consider the rating agency's maximization problem. The rating agency's profits consist of the product of the fee and ratings demand. It solves the following problem:

$$\max_{\alpha, \phi} \left(\theta_H - \theta_L\right) \phi \tag{11}$$

subject to participation conditions for the entrepreneur and investors, limited liability, and feasibility conditions. The limited liability condition prevents the entrepreneur from having negative value at $t = 4$ in case the risky project is unsuccessful. Feasibility conditions ensure that required repayment is less than X and that α and θ (as well as any thresholds for θ) lie in the unit interval. The next result rules out public financing by unrated entrepreneurs.

Lemma 2 (unrated issues): *In equilibrium $\theta_{U} = \theta_{L}$ and no unrated entrepreneurs raise financing.*

Lemma 2 arises because the willingness of rated customers to pay is higher when unrated entrepreneurs cannot enter the market. Whenever unrated entrepreneurs would want to raise financing, the rating agency has a profitable deviation. The entrepreneur's participation threshold, θ_{L}, exhibits the following comparative statics:

Lemma 3 (rating demand): *Without private lending, the rating threshold defined by the lowest type purchasing a rating, θ_{L}, is increasing in α and ϕ and decreasing in X.*

This result describes the influence of rating informativeness on the marginal ratings customer. Without private lending, only the lowest rated entrepreneur is a marginal rating customer. This entrepreneur prefers uninformative ratings to pool with high-quality entrepreneurs, and entrepreneurs with quality $\theta > \theta_{L}$ always purchase a rating.

Proposition 1 (baseline solution): *When a high cost of private borrowing rules out private financing ($\theta_{H} = 1$): (i) the rating agency chooses $\alpha^{*} = 0$ and (ii) there is a fee threshold ϕ' such that demand for ratings drops to zero for $\phi > \phi'$ because unrated public borrowing becomes possible. (iii) There is an associated project return X' such that for $X \geq X'$, the rating agency sets $\phi^{*} = \phi'$, and for $X < X'$ it sets $\phi^{*} < \phi'$.*

Proposition 1 describes conditions for both corner and interior solutions for the fee. The solution for the fee depends on a demand discontinuity (at ϕ') that arises because increasing the fee beyond ϕ' would allow unrated entrepreneurs to borrow. This result arises in the absence of viable outside options relative to public financing with a rating. The first part of the result is a corner solution for rating informativeness and is similar to Lizzeri's result (1999) about pooling of rated entrepreneurs.

The second part of the result suggests that there is a discontinuity in the entrepreneurs' willingness to pay that arises when unrated entrepreneurs become good enough, on average, to borrow from public lenders. To understand this discontinuity, consider the behavior of the marginal rating customer, who is indifferent between purchasing a rating and investing in the safe project without purchasing a rating. As the price of a rating increases, the rating threshold (which defines the quality of this marginal customer) also increases, raising the average quality of entrepreneurs who do not purchase a rating.

If it increases enough, unrated entrepreneurs may be able to raise financing by offering $R^{\mathrm{U}} < X$. As unrated access to public financing emerges, the baseline equilibrium from the first part of the solution unravels, and the rating agency makes zero profits. This is illustrated in Figure 3. If unrated entrepreneurs were unable to raise financing for $\phi > \phi'$, there would still be positive rating demand. The rating agency is constrained by the effect of its fee on the entrepreneur's ability to borrow without a rating.

I now modify the solution in Proposition 1 by considering a reduction in P, for example, from a lending supply shock. If P is low enough, a set of entrepreneurs with quality $\theta \in [\theta_{\mathrm{H}}, 1]$ chooses not to purchase a rating and raises financing from private lenders. Additionally, entrepreneurs with quality $\theta \in [\theta_{\mathrm{HU}}, \theta_{\mathrm{H}}]$ purchase a rating, but choose private financing if the rating is unfavorable. Their expected payoff if they purchase a rating is:

$$X - K + A - \phi - (1 - \alpha)P \tag{12}$$

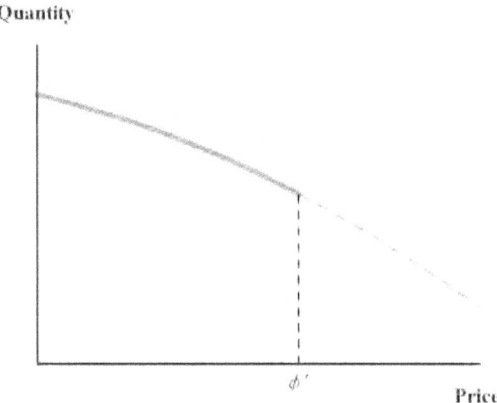

Figure 3: Proposition 1: demand discontinuity at ϕ'

The demand curve of the rating agency discontinuously drops to zero because of the ability of unrated entrepreneurs to raise capital. As the quantity demanded, $1 - \theta_{\text{L}}$, decreases, the quality of the average unrated entrepreneur increases. For $\phi > \phi'$, unrated access to public financing leads to zero ratings demand.

while if they borrow from private lenders, their payoff is $X - K + A - P$. Comparing this payoff with that in Equation (12) suggests these entrepreneurs will never purchase a rating if $\phi > 0$ and $\alpha = 0$.

Proposition 2 (informative ratings): *There is a private borrowing cost P' such that for $P < P'$, the rating agency sets $\alpha^* = \phi/P$.*

When using informative ratings to compete with private lenders, the rating agency loses some low-quality customers (because the low threshold for purchasing a rating, θ_{L}, is increasing in informativeness). It trades off losing those customers against losing some high-quality customers; losing high-quality customers also indirectly reduces the number of low-quality customers, by reducing the value of pooling. Proposition 2 suggests that the emergence of competition from private lenders for high-quality borrowers leads the rating agency to make ratings informative; this result forms the basis for empirical tests of the model in Section 5.

4.2 Unsolicited ratings

In this section, I consider the rating agency's incentives to issue unsolicited ratings. I modify the time line in Figure 1 to allow the rating agency to choose informativeness α_u for unsolicited ratings. As with solicited ratings, I assume that unsolicited ratings either reveal θ or reveal nothing about the entrepreneur, and that the rating agency can set informativeness without cost.

However, unlike solicited ratings, unsolicited ratings do not convey the borrower's rating purchase decision. Investors already know this decision, so unsolicited ratings that are uninformative cannot influence investor beliefs unless the rating agency chooses a disclosure policy for unsolicited ratings that depends on entrepreneur quality. Such a disclosure policy imparts information into unsolicited ratings even if $\alpha_u = 0$ (because investors' beliefs depend on the disclosure policy), which amounts to making unsolicited ratings informative.

I focus on the simple case in which the rating agency commits to producing unsolicited ratings if entrepreneurs do not purchase them. This allows me to rule out $\alpha_u^* = 0$ in some cases, and illustrates the intuition behind results in this section: if the purpose of unsolicited ratings is to prevent unrated borrowing, such ratings must contain some information.

Because unsolicited ratings increase the outside option for low-quality entrepreneurs, they reduce the fee the rating agency can charge for a rating:

Lemma 4 (cannibalization): *The ratings threshold θ_L is increasing in α_u.*

Lemma 4 illustrates a cost of unsolicited ratings for the rating agency: since they increase the outside option of unrated firms, they reduce demand for solicited ratings. Figure 4 illustrates financing thresholds for the model without competition from private lenders and with unsolicited ratings. The unsolicited rating threshold θ_{UN} is defined by the lowest-quality entrepreneur who can raise financing with an unsolicited rating.

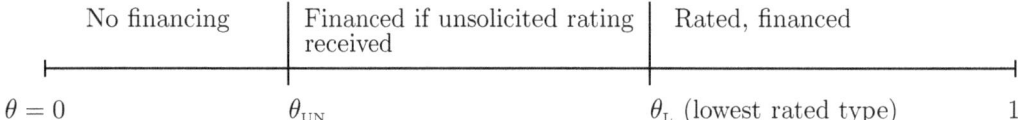

Figure 4: Entrepreneur participation with unsolicited ratings

This figure illustrates financing regions in equilibrium with unsolicited ratings. Using unsolicited ratings allows the rating agency to charge higher fees, which increases the quality of its lowest paying customer, θ_{L}. Unsolicited ratings allow entrepreneurs with quality $\theta \in [\theta_{\mathrm{UN}}, \theta_{\mathrm{L}}]$ to raise financing if they receive an unsolicited rating. If these entrepreneurs do not receive an unsolicited rating, they are pooled with unrated entrepreneurs.

Next, I show that unsolicited ratings allow the rating agency to sustain ratings demand for $\phi > \phi'$, preventing entrepreneurs that have neither solicited nor unsolicited ratings from public borrowing by reducing the average quality of unrated entrepreneurs.

Proposition 3 (unsolicited ratings): *Unsolicited ratings allow the rating agency to charge $\phi > \phi'$, where ϕ' is the fee threshold described in Proposition 1, when $\alpha_u > 0$. When the rating agency's optimal fee is $\phi^* < \phi'$, no unsolicited ratings are produced and results are identical to those in Proposition 1.*

The portion of the rating agency's demand curve that requires unsolicited ratings is illustrated using dashed lines in Figure 5, which describes the effect of an increase in X on the rating agency's choice of fee and use of unsolicited ratings. The fee threshold that allows unrated entrepreneurs to access public financing is ϕ'; increases in the fee beyond ϕ' require unsolicited ratings to prevent unrated access to public financing.

My explanation for the use of unsolicited ratings can accommodate allowing entrepreneurs to hide their ratings or allowing the rating agency to choose which unsolicited ratings to disclose. From the perspective of the rating agency, unsolicited ratings are used to influence investor beliefs and prevent unrated access to public borrowing; it succeeds if investors be-

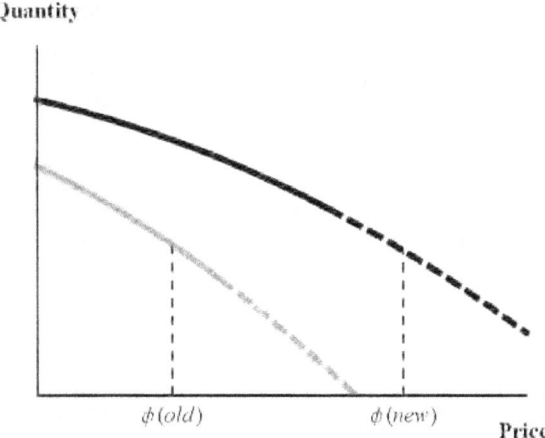

Figure 5: Increase in X leads to higher fee and unsolicited ratings
This figure illustrates how an increase in X can lead from equilibrium without unsolicited ratings to equilibrium with unsolicited ratings. The gray line is the rating agency's demand curve when X is low; the black line is the rating agency's demand curve with higher X. The dashed portion of each demand curve is only feasible with unsolicited ratings, which are necessary to prevent unrated firms from borrowing. When X is low, demand is more sensitive to the fee and the rating agency sets $\phi(old) < \phi'$. When X is high, the rating agency prefers $\phi(new) > \phi'$, but must use unsolicited ratings to prevent unrated entrepreneurs from borrowing.

lieve unrated entrepreneurs have low enough quality. Unsolicited ratings allow the rating agency to manipulate beliefs about unrated firms, preventing them from accessing public markets.

4.3 Productivity shifts and underinvestment

In this section, I analyze the impact of sudden changes to expected productivity. While such changes may also affect the distribution of entrepreneur types and value of assets in place, I restrict attention to productivity shocks that represent an increase to X, holding other variables fixed. There are two effects of a productivity shock: an increase to X lowers the ratings threshold, and reduces the sensitivity of rating customers to the fee, leading to a higher equilibrium fee. As illustrated in Figure 5, change in X can lead to equilibrium with unsolicited ratings.

With fixed K, X can be interpreted as a measure of expected productivity. Demand for ratings is less elastic when expected productivity is high, because the willingness to pay

20

of the marginal entrepreneur is less sensitive to the fee. Thus, Proposition 3 suggests that production of unsolicited ratings is pro-cyclical. During good times, the rating agency uses unsolicited ratings to prevent unrated borrowing, allowing it to charge higher fees.

Due to a higher ratings threshold, rated issues have lower default probability when productivity is low. Additionally, there is less variation in rated firm quality, as the threshold for ratings is higher. I define overinvestment as lost value arising from investment in NPV-negative firms, and underinvestment as value foregone from firms with positive-NPV projects that are unable to obtain financing.

NPV-neutral entrepreneurs have quality $\theta_0 \equiv K/X$. For $\theta_0 < \theta_L$, over-investment is:

$$\int_{\theta_L}^{\theta_0} (K - \theta X) \, d\theta \tag{13}$$

while otherwise ($\theta_0 \geq \theta_L$), under-investment is:

$$\int_{\theta_0}^{\theta_L} (\theta X - K)(1 - \alpha_u) \, d\theta. \tag{14}$$

The second term in Equation (14) arises from additional entrepreneurs who receive unsolicited ratings. Unsolicited ratings lead to underinvestment (relative to a setting with no unsolicited ratings). This is because of entrepreneurs with positive-NPV projects who do not receive unsolicited ratings and are unable to raise financing as a result.

Proposition 4 (dampening): *The rating agency dampens the effect of shocks to X on public lending.*

Proposition 4 suggests the rating agency dampens the effect of shocks to X on public lending. Because demand is more sensitive to price in bad times, the rating agency allows more entrepreneurs into public markets by reducing its fee. Similarly, when X is high, the rating agency increases fees. As illustrated in Figure 5, this leads to an increase in the

21

quantity demanded and a reduction in the rating threshold. The model suggests that a large increase in X can lead to equilibrium with unsolicited ratings. However, such an equilibrium will feature underinvestment:

Proposition 5 (underinvestment): *Equilibrium with unsolicited ratings features weakly higher underinvestment than equilibrium without unsolicited ratings.*

Unsolicited ratings allow higher fees, and benefit recipients. However, they allow extraction of surplus from rated entrepreneurs by the rating agency, and result in underinvestment during good times.

5   Data and methodology

The model suggests ratings should be informative for two reasons. First, informative ratings prevent defection of high-quality customers to private borrowing. Second, unsolicited ratings allow the rating agency to charge paying customers higher fees by preventing unrated public borrowing. Tests of the model focus on the rating agency's strategic use of informative ratings in response to competition from private lenders.

Proposition 2 suggests a critical value exists for P, the cost of private borrowing relative to that of public borrowing. If this relative cost becomes low, the model predicts the rating agency will make ratings informative. In practice, this relative cost is difficult to measure because of difficulties in separately identifying demand and supply, and because we observe incomplete measures of total private lending. A proxy for the cost is the relative supply of private vs. public lending.

I argue that the Riegle-Neal Act of 1994 and collapse of Drexel in 1999 allow identification of a positive shift in the relative supply of private vs. public lending. Each event increased competition from private lenders for a subset of borrowers. This allows for comparison of effects relative to a group of unaffected borrowers.

The collapse of Drexel led to a temporary shutdown in the public high-yield debt market without having a similar impact on the investment-grade market. Even if the supply of private lending decreased after the Drexel collapse, it is unlikely that it decreased for investment-grade borrowers in the same proportion as it decreased for high-yield borrowers. Following Drexel's collapse, I expect ratings to become more informative for high-yield entrepreneurs. The Riegle-Neal Act also led to a positive shift in the relative supply of private vs. public lending. By allowing interstate branching, it opened national credit markets to young issuers who were otherwise constrained to local borrowing (Zarutskie, 2006). Following this legislation, I expect ratings to become more informative for young issuers.

5.1 Data sources

Data for this project come from several sources. Firm-level accounting data are taken from Standard & Poor's Compustat Backtest Database Packages. These data are supplemented with the Compustat Industrial tables as well as the CRSP/Compustat Merged Database maintained by the Center for Research in Securities Prices (CRSP). The primary source for issuance data is Thomson Financial's Securities Data Corporation (SDC) database, which I supplement with data from the Securities and Exchange Commission's (SEC) Registered Offering Statistics tape and the CUSIP master file maintained by Standard & Poor's. SDC contains issue-level ratings data for major ratings agencies, and issuer-level ratings data from Moody's; this data are supplemented with ratings data from Standard & Poor's RatingsXpress Database (RX) and the Mergent Fixed Income Securities Database (FISD). I also use CRSP security prices to estimate market model parameters for each issuer.

I use bond issuance data from SDC, which contains information on 248,631 non-convertible public debt issues in the United States between 1980 and 2009. My initial sample includes both straight public debt issues and debt issued under the SEC's Rule 144A. As discussed by Carey, Prowse, Rea and Udell (1993) and Carey (1998), Rule 144A debt offerings are technically private placements but share many similarities with public issues.[8] From this sample, I exclude federal credit agency, sovereign, supra-national, mortgage, emerging-market, asset-backed, and non-dollar denominated deals.

Using the Fama French 12 industry definitions, I exclude financial firms and regulated utilities (Fama-French industries 8 and 11). Removing floating-rate debt and issues where the issuer had over 10 separate debt issuances on a single day leaves 61,949 issues (of these, 50,679 are straight public debt issues and the rest are issued under the SEC's Rule 144A). Matching with Compustat data and aggregating multiple issues on the same day by the same issuer yields the final sample of 7,396 issues. Of these, 5,748 are straight debt issues and 1,648 were issued under Rule 144A. The sample selection process is summarized in Table 2.

5.2   Description of variables

It is important that the accounting data I match to my sample were publicly available when each deal was priced. Since Compustat historical quarterly data are adjusted for restatements, I use the Compustat Backtest Database Packages to identify firm-level accounting data that were available at the time of each issue. I focus on the Point-in-Time History (PIT) file and the Unrestated Quarterly (URQ) file. Since the PIT file tracks restatements over time, I use the first observation in this file for each datadate. In the event a variable is missing from this dataset, I next look for the variable in URQ. If it is also missing there, I use the value for that variable from Compustat Industrial Tables if available, since it is unlikely to have been restated and be missing from the other two datasets.

My firm-level analysis focuses on variables related to the unobserved credit quality of the firm. These include measures of cash, cash flow, profitability, fixed assets, leverage (book and

---

[8]These similarities include having similar covenants and being underwritten. Rule 144A offerings also tend to be rated, while traditional private debt issues are frequently unrated.

market), and the ratio of book value to market value for both assets and shareholder's equity. For each variable, I include both the most recent value available at the time of the debt issue, as well as the mean and variance from quarterly data for the past 4 years. Table 3 provides details on how variables are constructed, and I present sample summary statistics in Table 4.

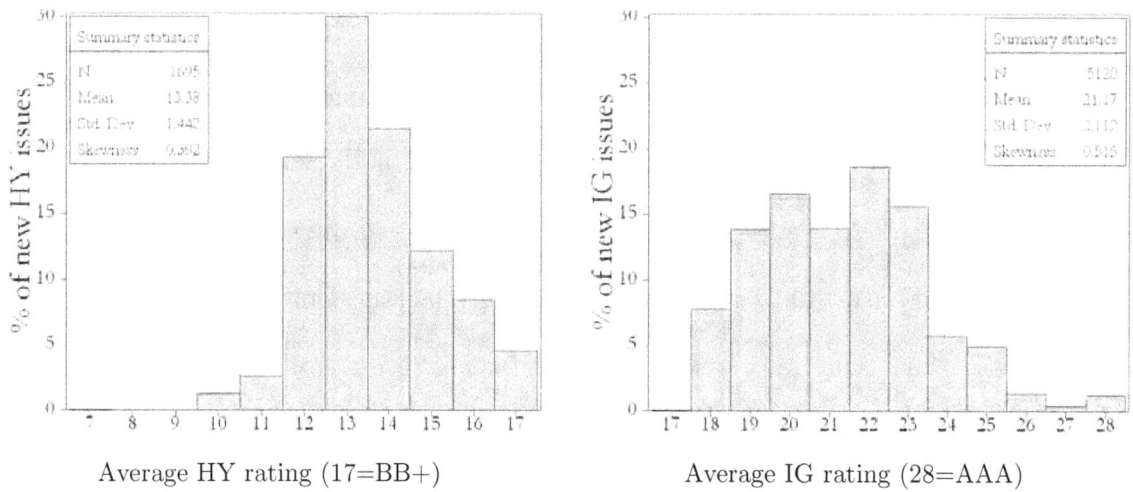

Average HY rating (17=BB+)   Average IG rating (28=AAA)

Figure 6: Distribution of ratings for high-yield and investment-grade issues
This figure illustrates the distribution of ratings for public debt issuers. The chart on the left is a histogram of ratings for high-yield debt issuers, while that on the right is for investment-grade issuers. A rating is defined as the average of numerical ratings by major rating agencies for a bond issue, where numbers are assigned to each rating class in ascending order following Becker and Milbourn (2010). The highest rating category is AAA; issues with average ratings below 17 are high-yield issues, those with average ratings above 17 are investment-grade issues. Each histogram displays the within-group, rather than across-group, distribution of ratings for issuers of public debt by US non-financial issuers between 1980 and 2009, that are matched to Compustat accounting data. Results of the sample selection process are presented in Table 2.

I follow Becker and Milbourn's (2010) numerical conversion of categorical ratings data: ratings are assigned numbers from 28 (AAA or 'extremely strong') to 4 (C or 'significantly speculative'). Only one new issue is assigned a rating below 9 in my sample. When issues are rated by more than one agency, I use the average rating. The sample distributions of the average rating for both high-yield and investment-grade issuers are summarized in Figure 6.

5.3 The informativeness of ratings

To test the hypothesis relating the informativeness of ratings to competition from private lenders, I require an information measure related to new issues that is relevant for pricing. I focus on pricing of new issues, rather than analyzing upgrades, downgrades, or default outcomes, for several reasons. Measuring informativeness using default outcomes is complicated by assessment of whether default was anticipated and because of timing differences between rating dates and default outcomes. Additionally, most of the rating agency's rating-related income comes from fees on new issues, rather than from ongoing maintenance fees (White, 2001). My measure extracts the information level in ratings from yield spreads. This approach has the advantage of directly estimating investors' expectations about rating quality.

Previous literature offers a variety of rating determination models that can be summarized by the rating prediction equation:

$$r_{i,b,t} = f(X_{i,b,t}) + \varepsilon_{i,b,t} \tag{15}$$

where issuers are indexed by i, issues (bonds) by b, time by t, and $X_{i,b,t}$ is a vector of firm-level and bond-level characteristics. Typical issue-level variables include the seniority of debt, its maturity, whether it was registered via SEC Rule 415 (shelf registration), is lease-related, or syndicated. Several previous studies discussed in Section 2 use models based on Equation (15) to predict ratings for issues or issuers, measure time trends, and explore cross-sectional variation in ratings determination. As noted by Kaplan and Urwitz (1979) and Kraft (2011), estimation of Equation (15) using OLS delivers results very close to results obtained using other methods (for example, results from ordered probit estimation). A concern with (15) is that ratings can also be driven by unobservable firm variables that also relate to access to credit. To address this concern, I include the firm's previous issuer-level rating as a control variable.

I also control for observable characteristics of the issue and issuer. The measure of informativeness I analyze relies on the following yield spread (YS) regression:

$$YS_{i,b,t} = \alpha_0 + \alpha_1 r_{i,b,t} + \gamma' X_{i,b,t} + \eta_{i,b,t} \tag{16}$$

I interpret the estimate of α_1 from Equation (16) as an aggregate measure of ratings informativeness. It can be interpreted as the cost of one rating point. I estimate Equation (16) both in a pooled regression context and year by year, to obtain an average level of ratings informativeness over time. As Liu and Thakor (1984) point out, standard errors in Equation (16) are likely to be biased upwards because of the high correlation between the control variables ($\gamma' X_{i,b,t}$) and the rating ($r_{i,b,t}$). This suggests the standard errors I estimate are conservative.

5.4 The influence of capital supply on ratings informativeness

To relate informativeness to the relative supply of private vs. public lending, I analyze the Riegle-Neal Interstate Banking Act of 1994. Following Dick (2006) and Zarutskie (2006), I interpret the Riegle-Neal Act as a positive shock to private lending supply. By reducing barriers to interstate branching, this legislation increased the supply of bank lending for issuers constrained to local borrowing, without having a similar impact on the supply of public lending. Following Zarutskie (2006), I relate an issuer's age to its ability to borrow privately, assuming older firms were less influenced by this legislation due to preexisting access to national borrowing markets. I focus on young borrowers, whose first public security issuance was within five years. The distribution of issuer age in my sample is illustrated in Figure 7.

Let I^y be an indicator variable for a young firm (I define a young firm as one less than 5 years old). I measure the effect of the Riegle-Neal Act on rating informativeness by estimating the following regression:

$$YS_{i,b,t} = \beta_1 r * RN_t * I_{i,t}^y + \beta_2\, r * I_{i,t}^y + \beta_3 r RN_t + \beta_4 r + \beta_5 RN_t + \beta_6 I_{i,t}^y + \gamma' X_{i,b,t} + \eta_{i,b,t} \tag{17}$$

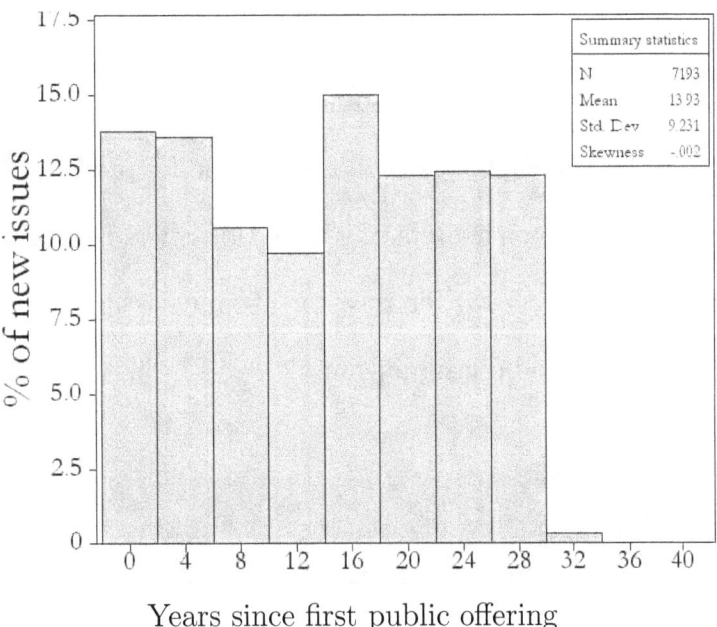

Figure 7: Histogram of public debt issuer age, 1980-2009

This histogram illustrates the age distribution of issuers of public debt by US nonfinancial issuers between 1980 and 2009, that are matched to Compustat accounting data. I define age as the number of years since the issuer's first public offering of any security in SDC. Results of the sample selection process are presented in Table 2.

where RN_t is an indicator variable for the post-legislation period and I drop subscripts i, b, t on the rating r for ease of exposition. The model predicts $\beta_1 < 0$ under the assumption that the Riegle-Neal Act increased the supply of private vs. public lending for young issuers.

Next, I analyze the collapse in 1989 of the high-yield market brought on by the bankruptcy of Drexel. As discussed by Lemmon and Roberts (2010), this collapse led to a temporary shutdown in the high-yield market after 1989. The model predicts the rating agency responds to such an event by increasing the informativeness of ratings for issuers who experienced an increase in the relative supply of private vs. public lending. To measure the influence of the Drexel collapse on ratings informativeness, I analyze a sample of high-yield issues during a 4-year window surrounding 1989. I estimate the following regression:

$$YS_{i,b,t} = \beta_1 I_{1989} * r_{i,b,t} + \beta_2 r_{i,b,t} + \beta_3 I_{1989} + \gamma' X_{i,b,t} + \nu_{i,b,t} \tag{18}$$

where I_{1989} is an indicator variable set to 1 during the post-1989 period. The coefficient of interest is β_1, which measures the influence of the credit rating on pricing during the post-1989 period, relative to this impact before 1989. The model predicts $\beta_1 < 0$. Because the shock to the supply of public financing affects high-yield issuers more than investment-grade issuers, I also estimate Equation (18) for investment-grade issues during the same period, and expect my estimate of β_1 to be insignificant.

6 Empirical results

My results suggest that when a subset of issuers experiences a positive shock to the relative supply of private vs. public lending, ratings for this subset of issuers become more informative. After the Drexel collapse, I find that ratings became more informative for high-yield issuers, but not for investment-grade issuers. Similarly, I find that ratings became more informative for young issuers following the Riegle-Neal Act, but not for older issuers. My results are robust to alternative window specifications: for each event, I show that my estimate of ratings informativeness decreases as a larger period of time is analyzed. I also test the counter-factual hypotheses that each event occurred during a different event year.

6.1 Aggregate ratings informativeness

Results of yield spread regressions from estimating Equation (16) annually are illustrated in Figure 8. This figure plots the coefficient on the rating in a regression of the yield spread on issue- and issuer-level control variables. The coefficient in Figure 8 is scaled by the annual average yield spread, so the level in Figure 8 can be interpreted as the percentage of the yield spread driven by unexplained variation in the credit rating.

These results suggest that, on average, one rating point costs borrowers between 20 and 30 basis points, slightly over 10% of the mean yield spread for my sample of 210 basis points. Figure 8 illustrates time series variation in the average informativeness for new corporate bond issues, and suggests there is substantial time-series variation in the cost of one rating point for new issuers. This cost reaches its highest level in 1991, following the Drexel collapse.

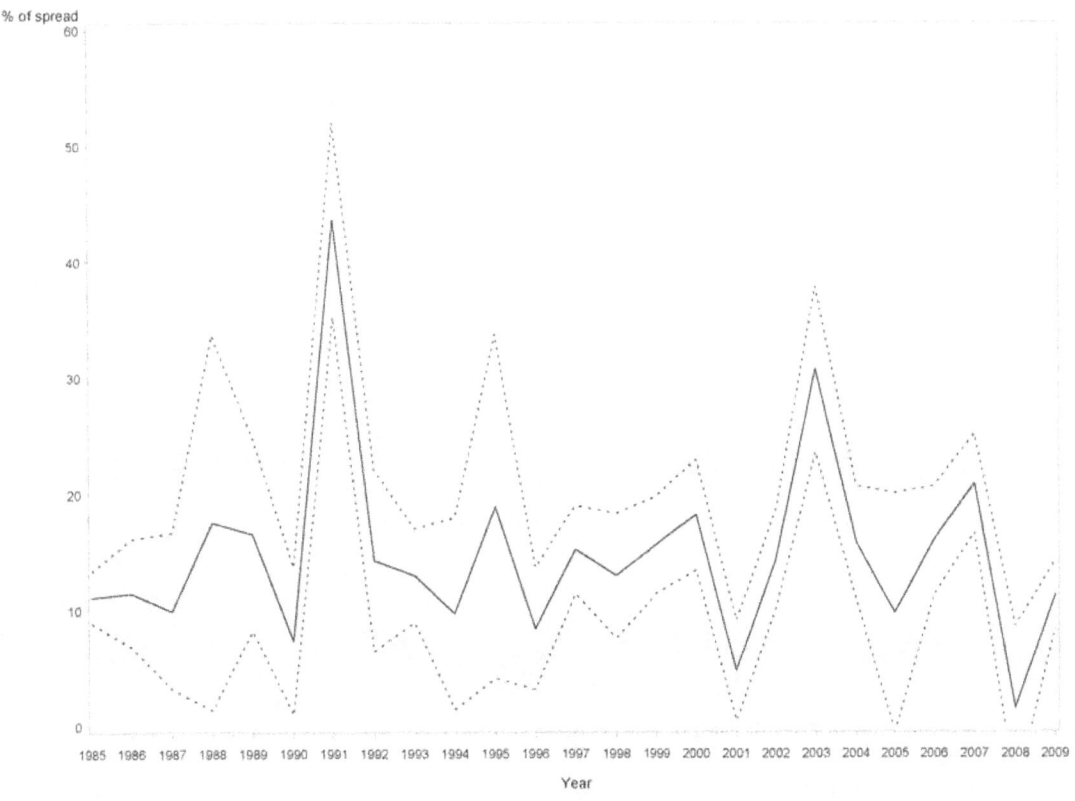

Figure 8: Estimated rating informativeness, 1985-2009

This figure illustrates the coefficient of the rating on annual regressions of the yield spread on the rating, issue-level and issuer-level control variables. Each year's estimate of α_1 from Equation 16 is scaled by the mean credit spread of all issues in that year. The dashed lines represent intervals of one standard error around each estimate. Each regression includes Fama French 12-industry fixed effects. The sample includes fixed-rate public debt issues by non-financial, non-utility issuers in the SDC New Issues Database, matched to Compustat accounting data. Details on the sample selection process are presented in Table 2.

Since I do not know the full information set of investors, it could be that the ratings I analyze contain less information than I estimate. Kraft (2011) relates off-balance sheet debt and other adjustments to ratings. I argue that these adjustments are not likely to influence my results for two reasons. First, a previous issuer-level rating, if available, likely incorporates similar information to adjustments made by the rating agency for off-balance sheet items. In unreported results, I estimate Equation (15). I find higher R^2 than Kraft's model (2011), suggesting off-balance sheet adjustments are correlated with my controls.

However, I acknowledge that off-balance sheet items may still affect investors' expectations about an issuer's rating.

6.2   The Riegle-Neal Act and rating informativeness

In Table 5, I present results from estimating Equation (17) over a 4-year window around passage of the Riegle-Neal Act. Following Zarutskie, I compare bond issues before 1994 with issues after 1994. The coefficient of interest is the (boxed) estimated coefficient on the interaction of the rating, RN and an indicator variable for age less than 5 years ($\hat{\beta}_1$). As expected, this estimated coefficient is negative and significant in each specification.

To confirm that my results relate to young issuers, rather than to issuers in other age groups, I also estimate Equation (17) using an indicator variable for issuers from other age groups. I cannot reject the null hypothesis that there was no change in rating informativeness for other age groups. In Table 6, I report results from using an indicator variable for middle-aged issuers (those whose age is between 10 and 15 years). The only difference in methodology for results reported in Table 6 and those reported in Table 5 is a different definition of the age variable. My estimate of β_1 is insignificant in each specification in Table 6. The results reported in Tables 5 and 6 suggest ratings became more informative for younger issuers, but not for older issuers, after nationwide passage of the Riegle-Neal Act.

6.3   The Drexel collapse and rating informativeness

Results from estimating Equation (18) are presented in Table 7. The coefficient of interest is the (boxed) estimated coefficient on the interaction of the rating and the indicator variable for the post-Drexel period ($\hat{\beta}_1$). My estimate of this coefficient is negative and significant, suggesting ratings became more informative for high-yield issuers following 1989. I estimate Equation (18) using both the log of the yield spread (models 1 and 3) and the level (models 2 and 4) as the dependent variable. I present results that treat issues by the same issuer on the same day as separate observations (models 1 and 2). Since these observations are likely correlated, I also present results from estimating Equation (18) using a sample that aggregates issues by the same issuer on the same day.

The coefficient on the interaction of the rating and indicator for the post-collapse period suggests that the cost of an unexpected rating was between 20 and 24 basis points higher for high-yield issuers after the Drexel collapse. This is approximately half of the average cost of an unexpected rating point during this period (based on the estimated coefficient on the rating). My estimate of these coefficients include year and industry fixed effects, and control for the issuer's prior rating as well as for issuer- and issue-level variables.

Table 8 presents results of estimating Equation (18) for investment-grade issuers. My estimate of β_1 in each model in Table 8 is insignificant, suggesting ratings did not become more informative following the Drexel collapse for investment-grade issuers. This result is consistent with with the Drexel collapse affecting high-yield issuers more than investment-grade issuers. I follow the same methodology for reporting results in Tables 7 and 8, and cannot reject the null hypothesis that $\beta_1 = 0$ in models (1)-(4).

Results in Tables 7 and 8 suggest that the Drexel collapse led to an increase in the informativeness of credit ratings for high-yield issuers, but not for investment-grade issuers. This is consistent with a higher influence of the Drexel collapse on the relative supply of private vs. public capital for high-yield issuers, due to increased competition from private lenders.

6.4   Robustness tests

While my results in Section 6 are significant, it could be that these results are driven by the choice of the period length I consider. Alternatively, my results could arise from variation in informativeness unrelated to the specific events I analyze. To account for these possibilities, I analyze the robustness of my results to alternative window lengths, and test the counterfactual hypothesis that each event occurred at a different time.

Panel A of Table 9 illustrates the effect of changing the analysis period surrounding the date of nationwide passage of the Riegle-Neal Act. Consistent with the results in Table 10, I find stronger results for smaller windows. The Riegle-Neal Act appears to have had a lasting impact on ratings informativeness for young firms, as I continue to find significant results as the length of the analysis period is increased to six years. The coefficient on the interaction of the rating and the post-event period remains negative.

Panel B of Table 9 presents results from estimating Equation (17) using different event years. Using a four-year window, I find significant results for the coefficient on the interaction of the rating, indicator for young firm, and post-shock period under the assumption that the shock occurred in 1993 or 1994. No other year produces a significant result. Interestingly, results are stronger for the hypothesis that the Riegle-Neal Act occurred in 1993, which suggests the legislation was anticipated prior to its formal passage in 1994.

In Panel A of Table 10, I present results from changing the analysis period surrounding the year of the Drexel collapse. Consistent with the hypothesis that the collapse was unexpected, I find stronger results for smaller windows. A two-year window yields the largest results, and results become insignificant when the window length is increased to five years. The coefficient on the interaction of the rating and the indicator for post-event period remains negative in these specifications. However, the number of observations decreases quickly around the time of the Drexel collapse due to the resulting temporary shutdown of the high-yield market.

Panel B of Table 10 presents results from estimating Equation (18) using other years. I find significant results for the coefficient on the interaction of the rating and indicator for post-shock period under the assumption that the shock occurred in 1987, 1988, or 1989. These results are consistent with overlap of the four-year analysis period with the collapse of Drexel in 1989. Results for 1987, 1990, and 1991 are not significant.

7 Conclusion

This paper analyzes a credit rating agency's strategic use of information in corporate credit ratings. The model relates informative credit ratings to competition between public and private lenders facilitated by the rating agency. Tests of the model suggest ratings contain more information when public lenders face increased competition from private lenders. The model also suggests unsolicited ratings raise the level of the lowest-quality solicited ratings during good times. This allows the rating agency to charge higher fees and extract monopolist rents, which can lead to underinvestment. Results shed new light on the gatekeeper role of the ratings sector, and on the nature of competition between public and private lenders.

References

[1] Amato, J. and C. Furfine, 2004. "Are credit ratings procyclical?" *Journal of Banking and Finance*, 28, 2641-2677.

[2] Bar-Isaac, H. and J. Shapiro, 2012. "Ratings quality over the business cycle," Working paper, New York University.

[3] Becker, B. and T. Milbourn, 2011. "How did increased competition affect credit ratings?" *Journal of Financial Economics*, 493-514.

[4] Blume, Lim and MacKinlay, C. 2006. "The declining quality of U.S. corporate debt: Myth and reality?" *Journal of Finance*, 53, 1389-1413.

[5] Bolton, P., X. Freixas, and J. Shapiro, 2012. "The credit ratings game," *Journal of Finance*, 67, 85-111.

[6] Cantor, R., and F. Packer, 1994. "The credit rating industry," *Federal Reserve Board of New York Quarterly Review / Summer-Fall*, p. 5.

[7] Carey, M., 1998. "Credit risk in private debt portfolios," *Journal of Finance*, 53, 1363-1387.

[8] Carey, M., S. Prowse, J. Rea and G. Udell, 1993. "The economics of the private placement market," *Federal Reserve Board Staff Study*.

[9] Diamond, D., 1991. "Monitoring and reputation: The choice between bank loans and directly placed debt," *Journal of Political Economy*, 99, 689-721.

[10] Dichev, I., and J. Piotroski, 2001. "The long run stock returns following bond ratings changes," *Journal of Finance*, 61, 173-203.

[11] Dick, A., 2006. "Nationwide branching and its impact on market structure, quality, and bank performance," *Journal of Business*, 79, 567-592.

[12] Doherty, N., A. Kartasheva and R. Phillips, 2012. "Information effect of entry into credit ratings market: The case of insurers' ratings," *Journal of Financial Economics*, 106, 308-330.

[13] Ederington, L., 1985. "Classification models and bond ratings," *Financial Review*, 20, 237-262.

[14] Faulkender, M. and M. Petersen, 2006, "Does the source of capital affect capital structure", *The Review of Financial Studies*, 19, 45-79.

[15] Faure-Grimaud, A., E. Peyrache and L. Quesada, 2009. "The ownership of ratings," *RAND Journal of Economics*, 40, 234-257.

[16] Fulghieri, P., G. Strobl, H. Xia, 2013. "The economics of solicited and unsolicited credit ratings," Working paper, University of North Carolina.

[17] Hand, J., R. Holthausen and R. Leftwich., 1992. "The effect of bond rating agency announcements on bond and stock prices," *Journal of Finance*, 47, 733-752.

[18] Holthausen, R., and R. Leftwich, 1986. "The effect of bond rating changes on common stock prices," *Journal of Financial Economics*, 17, 57-89.

[19] Horrigan, J., 1966. "The determination of long-term credit standing with financial ratios," *Journal of Accounting Research*, 4, 44-62.

[20] Hull, J., M. Predescu, and A. White, 2004, "The relationship between credit default swap spreads, bond yields, and credit rating announcements," *Journal of Financial Economics*, 40, 2789-2811.

[21] Jaffee, D., 2009, Comment on "Rating the raters," by Mathis, J., J. McAndrews and J. Rochet, *Journal of Monetary Economics*, 56, 675-677.

[22] Jorion, P., Z. Liu and C. Shi, 2005. "Informational effects of regulation FD: evidence from rating agencies," *Journal of Financial Economics*, 76, 309-330.

[23] Kaplan, R. and G. Urwitz, 1979, "Statistical models of bond ratings: A methodological inquiry," *Journal of Business*, 52, 231-261.

[24] Kliger, D. and O. Sarig, 2000, "The information value of bond ratings," *Journal of Finance*, 60, 2879-2902.

[25] Kraft, P., 2011, "Rating agency adjustments to GAAP financial statements and their effect on ratings and bond yields," Working Paper, New York University.

[26] Leary, M. , 2009, "Bank loan supply, lender choice, and corporate capital structure," *Journal of Finance*, 64, 1143-1185.

[27] Leland, H. and D. Pyle, 1977, "Informational asymmetries, financial structure and financial intermediation," *Journal of Finance*, 32, 371-387.

[28] Lemmon, M. and M. Roberts, 2010, "The response of corporate financing and investment to changes in the supply of credit," *Journal of Financial and Quantitiative Analysis*, 45, 555-587.

[29] Liu, P. and A. Thakor, 1984, "Interest yields, credit ratings, and economic characteristics of state bonds: An empirical analysis," *Journal of Money, Credit and Banking*, 16, 344-351.

[30] Lizzeri, A., 1999, "Information revelation and certification intermediaries," *RAND Journal of Economics*, 30, 214-231.

[31] Mathis, J., J. McAndrews and J. Rochet, 2009, "Rating the raters: are reputation concerns powerful enough to discipline the rating agencies?" *Journal of Monetary Economics*. 56, 657-674.

[32] Opp, C. and M. Opp, and Harris, M., 2013. "Rating agencies in the face of regulation," *Journal of Financial Economics*, 108, 46-61.

[33] Rajan, R., 1992, "Insiders and outsiders: The choice between informed and arm's-length debt," *Journal of Finance*, 47, 1367-1400.

[34] Sangiorgi, F., J. Sokobin and C. Spatt, 2009, "Credit-rating shopping, selection and the equilibrium structure of ratings," Working paper, Stockholm School of Economics.

[35] Sharpe, S., 1990, "Asymmetric information, bank lending and implicit contracts: A stylized model of customer relationships," *Journal of Finance*, 45, 1069-1087.

[36] Skreta, V. and L. Veldkamp, 2009, "Ratings shopping and asset complexity: A theory of ratings inflation," *Journal of Monetary Economics*, 56, 678-695.

[37] Sylla, R., 2001, "A Historical Primer on the Business of Credit Ratings," Working Paper, New York University.

[38] White, L., 2001, "The credit rating industry: An industrial organization analysis," Working Paper #CLB-01-001, New York University.

[39] Zarutskie, R., 2006, "Evidence on the effects of bank competition on firm borrowing and investment," *Journal of Financial Economics*, 81, 503-537.

A Proofs

Proof of Lemma 1: First, note that the benefit of investing less than A in the risky project decreases in the issuer's quality. If any issuer invests less than A, high-quality issuers would deviate and borrow less. The only possible beliefs about an issuer that invests less than A are that the issuer has the lowest possible type: $\theta = 0$. The result follows from noting that financing would never be possible for such an issuer. ∎

Proof of Lemma 2: When $0 < \theta_{\mathrm{L}} < 1$, where without unrated borrowing, the marginal issuer is indifferent between purchasing a rating and investing in the safe project. Consider $0 < \theta_{\mathrm{U}} < \theta_{\mathrm{L}} < 1$. Compared with the case where unrated issuers cannot borrow, this reduces the attractiveness of purchasing a rating, increasing θ_{L}. However, such an increase also reduces θ_{U}, because the average quality of unrated issuers increases. This process continues, ruling out $\theta_{\mathrm{L}} < 1$, which suggests that ratings demand is zero when $\theta_{\mathrm{U}} < \theta_{\mathrm{L}}$ and $\phi > 0$. ∎

Proof of Lemma 3: Comparing Equations (6) and (9), the minimum quality for seeking public financing with an informative rating is $\theta_0 = K/X$. If $\theta_{\mathrm{L}} > \theta_0$, all issuers who seek ratings seek financing. Otherwise, those with quality $\theta \in [\theta_{\mathrm{L}}, \theta_0)$ seek financing only if they receive a favorable rating. Their expected profits from a rating are:

$$\alpha(A - \phi) + (1 - \alpha)\theta\left[X - \frac{2(K - A + \phi)}{\theta_{\mathrm{H}} + \theta_{\mathrm{L}}}\right] \tag{19}$$

Comparing Equation (19) with A, solving at equality for $\theta = \theta_{\mathrm{L}}$, and taking the positive root yields:

$$\theta_{\mathrm{L}} = \frac{\Gamma + \sqrt{4X(1 - \alpha)(\alpha\phi\theta_{\mathrm{H}} + (1 - \alpha)(\theta_{\mathrm{H}}A)) + \Gamma^2}}{2X(1 - \alpha)}; \theta_{\mathrm{L}} < \theta_0 \tag{20}$$

where $\Gamma \equiv (1 - \alpha)(2\phi + 2K - A + \theta_{\mathrm{H}}X)$. In this case, the minimum rated issuer is NPV-negative. For $\theta_{\mathrm{L}} > \theta_0$, and all issuers who seek ratings enter the market. Expected profits from getting a rating are:

$$\alpha(\theta X - K - A + \phi) + (1 - \alpha)\theta\left[X - \frac{2(K - A + \phi)}{\theta_{\mathrm{H}} + \theta_{\mathrm{L}}}\right] \tag{21}$$

Comparing Equation (21) with A and solving at equality for $\theta = \theta_{\mathrm{L}}$ yields:

$$\theta_{\mathrm{L}} = \frac{\Gamma + \sqrt{4(\theta_{\mathrm{H}}\phi\alpha + \alpha K\theta_{\mathrm{H}} + (1 - \alpha)\theta_{\mathrm{H}}A) + \Gamma^2}}{2X}; \theta_{\mathrm{L}} \geq \theta_0 \tag{22}$$

where $\Gamma \equiv (2 - \alpha)(\phi + K) - (1 - \alpha)A - \theta_{\mathrm{H}}X$. The result follows from taking derivatives of Equations (20) and (22) with respect to α and ϕ. ∎

Proof of Proposition 1: Since high P rules out $\theta_{\mathrm{H}} < 1$, $\alpha^* = 0$ follows from Lemma 3. The maximum fee arises from the participation constraint of unrated issuers, who seek public financing if:

$$\theta \left[X - \frac{2(K-A)}{\theta_U + \theta_L} \right] \geq A \tag{23}$$

Solving Equation (23) at equality for $\theta = \theta_U$ (and taking the positive root) yields an expression for the threshold for raising public financing by unrated issuers.

$$\theta_U = \frac{2K - A - \theta_L X + \sqrt{4\theta_L AX + (2K - A - \theta_L X)^2}}{2X} \tag{24}$$

If $\theta_U < \theta_L$ entry by unrated issuers leads to unraveling of the solution in Proposition 1. θ_U decreases in θ_L, which increases in ϕ. Thus, we can solve for ϕ' by setting $\theta_U = \theta_L$:

$$\phi' = \frac{(1-\alpha)(K-A)(X-K)}{(2-\alpha)K - \alpha X} \tag{25}$$

It can be verified that $\phi > \phi'$ leads to $\theta_U > \theta_L$, and unrated issuers can raise public financing. The rating agency's first order condition is:

$$1 - \theta_L = \phi \frac{d\theta_L}{d\phi} \tag{26}$$

which can be solved for ϕ^*, which is increasing in X. X' is the value of X such that $\phi^* = \phi'$. The result follows from noting that demand drops to zero for $\phi^* > \phi'$ due to entry of unrated issuers. ∎

Proof of Proposition 2: Suppose $\theta_H < 1$ Since higher quality issuers prefer informative ratings, comparing Equations (7) and (8) yields the high threshold for unconditionally choosing public financing relative to private financing:

$$\theta_{HU} = \frac{(\theta_L + \theta_H)(K + P - A)}{2(\phi + K - A)} \tag{27}$$

For issuers with quality $\theta \in [\theta_L, \theta_H]$, paying ϕ must increase expected profits. Comparing Equation (12) with profits from private financing yields the participation condition for a high-quality issuer to purchase a rating:

$$\alpha P > \phi \tag{28}$$

When $\alpha = 0$, types $[\theta_{HU}, 1]$ do not purchase ratings, yielding:

$$\theta_H = \theta_{HU} = \frac{\theta_L(K + P - A)}{2\phi + K - A - P} < 1 \tag{29}$$

while for $\alpha > \phi/P$, $\theta_H = 1$. The rating agency's compares profits for $\alpha = 0$ to profits where $\alpha = \phi/P$. $\alpha > \phi/P$ is ruled out because given $\theta_H = 1$, demand for ratings is decreasing in θ_L. Profits are lower for $\theta_H < 1$: because of fee income lost from both high-quality and from low-quality issuers. Denote $\theta_H' \equiv \theta_H|_{\alpha=0} < 1$ the threshold for choosing private lending when ratings are uninformative. If $\alpha \geq \phi/B$, $\theta_H = 1$. However, θ_H also influences the behavior of the low-quality marginal issuer. The condition for the rating agency to include information is:

$$\left[\theta_{\mathrm{L}}|_{\alpha=\phi/P,\theta_{\mathrm{H}}=1} - \theta_{\mathrm{L}}|_{\alpha=0,\theta_{\mathrm{H}}=\theta'_{\mathrm{H}}}\right] \leq 1 - \theta_{\mathrm{HU}} \tag{30}$$

the result follows from substituting Equation (29) for θ_{H} and solving for P (yielding P').∎

Proof of Proposition 3: Suppose $X > X'$, so without the rating agency sets $\phi^* > \phi'$ if it can avoid the demand discontinuity discussed in Proposition 1. Let θ_{U} be defined as in Equation (24). To prevent unraveling, the rating agency must satisfy:

$$E[\theta|\mathrm{unrated}] < \frac{\theta_{\mathrm{L}}(\theta\mathrm{X} - \mathrm{A})}{\mathrm{K} - \mathrm{A}} \tag{31}$$

As production α_u is increased, issuers with neither solicited nor unsolicited ratings are more likely to have quality $\theta \in (\theta_{\mathrm{U}}, \theta_{\mathrm{UN}})$. Using Bayes' rule, their expected type of an unrated issuer is:

$$E[\theta|\mathrm{unrated}] = \frac{(1 - \alpha_u)(\theta_{\mathrm{U}}^2 + \theta_{\mathrm{L}}^2) - \alpha_u\theta_{\mathrm{UN}}^2}{2\left[\theta_{\mathrm{U}} - \theta_{\mathrm{L}}(1 - \alpha_u) - \alpha_u\theta_{\mathrm{UN}}\right]} \tag{32}$$

where the result follows from choosing α_u to satisfy Equation (31). Since the rating agency's profits for any $\phi'' \in (\phi', \phi^*)$ are higher than profits for $\phi < \phi'$, this result can obtain even with a cost for unsolicited ratings. ∎

Proof of Proposition 4: The demand curve is given by $\theta_{\mathrm{H}} - \theta_{\mathrm{L}}$. Since θ_{H} does not depend on X, the result follows from noting that $\frac{d^2\theta_{\mathrm{L}}(\cdot)}{d\phi dX} > 0$.∎

Proof of Proposition 5: Unsolicited ratings occur for $X > X'$. The result follows from comparing (22) and (24), since $\theta_{\mathrm{LU}} < \theta_{\mathrm{L}}$ when $X > X'$. ∎

Table 1: Notation summary for Section 4

X	Project success return (exogenous)
K	Capital required by project (exogenous)
A	Issuer's value for assets in place (exogenous)
P	Private lenders' required return (exogenous)
θ	Probability of project success (*quality* or *type* of issuer)
ϕ	Fee charged by rating agency for producing and disclosing signal
ϕ'	Fee level above which unrated issuers seek financing
X'	Project return associated with $\phi^* = \phi'$ in the baseline model
α	Informativeness of the rating
r	Rating generated by rating agency
Θ	Set of thresholds summarizing issuer participation
θ_{L}	Lowest type who purchases a rating
θ_{LU}	Lowest rated type who pursues public financing unconditional on rating
θ_{HU}	Highest rated type who pursues public financing unconditional on rating
θ_{H}	Highest rated type
θ_{U}	Threshold for entering market: lowest unrated type seeking financing
θ_{UN}	Minimum quality for which unsolicited ratings are disclosed
$R(r)$	Required debt repayment with rating r
R^{U}	Required debt repayment if unrated
R^{P}	Required debt repayment for private financing
α_u	Production level for unsolicited ratings
θ_0	Quality level such that issuer is NPV-neutral

Table 2: Sample selection procedure

This table summarizes results of the sample selection procedure for new debt issues described in Section 5. I begin with the set of all public debt issues from the SDC New Issues Database (master deal types D and R144D). From this initial public debt sample, I exclude federal credit agency and mortgage-related deals, as well issues from non-US issuers, issues that are not denominated in dollars, and issues of floating-rate debt. I also exclude issues by issuers with over 10 issues on a single day, since such issues by industrial companies are likely related to unusual financing events. These issues are then matched with unrestated quarterly issuer data from Compustat. I exclude financial issuers and utilities (using Fama-French 12 industry definitions) to obtain a final sample of 11,348 issues by nonfinancial industrial companies. I aggregate multiple issues by an issuer on the same day and present results with and without aggregation.

Selection rule	Number of deals			Principal Amount ($ Millions)		
	Total	Straight debt	Rule 144A	Total	Straight debt	Rule 144A
Initial debt sample	248,631	190,636	57,995	$33,534,671	$26,387,483	$7,147,188
Exclude federal agency/GSE/sovereign	131,018	73,219	57,799	20,170,211	13,075,777	7,094,434
Exclude mortgage (issue-type= MB)	121,059	73,219	47,840	19,490,918	13,075,777	6,415,141
Exclude emerging market (issue-type=EM)	120,188	72,966	47,222	19,339,289	13,016,938	6,322,351
Exclude asset-backed (issue-type= AB)	92,168	72,966	19,202	16,483,625	13,016,938	3,466,687
Dollar-denominated	91,588	72,547	19,041	16,118,842	12,742,883	3,375,959
Exclude issues without fixed-rate	63,833	52,075	11,758	11,111,511	8,804,827	2,306,684
Exclude issues with >10 deal(s) per day	61,949	50,679	11,270	10,976,313	8,705,781	2,270,533
Compustat match	21,601	18,632	2,969	5,559,854	4,655,609	904,245
Exclude non-US deals	20,352	17,548	2,804	5,122,880	4,288,550	834,330
SDC Rating data available	20,348	17,545	2,803	5,121,455	4,288,125	833,330
Exclude financials (FF12=11)	13,758	11,267	2,491	3,644,937	2,907,987	736,950
Exclude utilities (FF12=8)	11,348	9,054	2,294	3,233,383	2,563,020	670,363
Combine multiple issuances/day	7,396	5,748	1,648	3,233,383	2,563,020	670,363

42

Table 3: Variable definitions

The data sources and sample selection procedure are described in Section 5.2. I access the Compustat Unrestated Quarterly (URQ), Point in Time (PIT), and Fundamental Quarterly Table (Fundq) using Wharton Research Data Services (WRDS). Variable abbreviations refer to variable names in Fundq tables on WRDS. As discussed in Section 5.2, I search for each variable first in the PIT or URQ tables, since data in the Fundq table are adjusted for restatements. Quarterly values from cash flow statement (variable names ending in y), presented as year to date numbers, have been adjusted by subtracting the lagged quarterly value in fiscal quarters 2, 3, and 4.

Age	= (Date of first public offering (SDC) - issuedate)/365
Altman Z score	= 1.2(wcapq / atq) + 1.4(req/atq) + 3.3(oiadpq/atq)+ + 0.6(prccq*cshoq/ltq)+0.999*revtq/atq
Book assets	= atq
Callable	= Indicator(any part issue is callable) (SDC)
Cash	= Maximum of cheq,chq
Date of first public offering	= Minimum date in SDC for master deal type D, P, C
Datadate	= Date of accounting data in Compustat
Ebit	= Operating income after depreciation (oiadpq)
Ebitda	= Operating income before depreciation (oibdpq)
Fixed assets (PPE)	= ppentq (Property, plant and equipment at net book value)
Has prior rating	= Indicator(issuer-level rating in RX or FISD)
Interest expense	= xinty
Issuedate	= Date of security issue (SDC)
Leverage (book)	= (dlttq+dlcq) / atq
Leverage (market)	= (dlttq+dlcq) / (dlttq + dlcq + prccq*cshoq)
Market to book (assets)	= (prccq*cshoq+lseq-ceqq) / atq
Maturity	= Date of final maturity (SDC) - Issuedate
Principal	= Total principal amount all markets (SDC)
Rating	= Avg. new issue rating, ordered from 28 to 1 (SDC,RX, FISD)
Return on equity	= ni/ceq (Net income / book value of common equity)
Rule 144A	= Indicator(SDC master deal type = R144D)
Shelf registered	= Indicator(SDC flags deal as originating from rule 415 filing)
Subordinated	= Indicator(SDC flags deal as subordinated)
Syndicated	= Indicator(SDC flags deal as syndicated)
Yield spread	= Issue YTM - spread on treasury with same maturity (SDC)

Table 4: New issue summary statistics

This table reports summary statistics for new public debt issues that survive the sample selection procedure summarized in Table 2. Issuance data are taken from the Securities Data Corporation (SDC) New Issues Database, and are matched to the Compustat Backtest databases, as well as to Compustat Industrial Annual data. For each issue-level observation in Panel A, data are from quarterly filings that were publicly available before the issue date (and are not adjusted for subsequent restatement). Four-year average columns reflect averages of unrestated quarterly data over four years preceding each issue. Panel A summarizes issuer-level variables, while Panel B summarizes issue-level variables.

Panel A: Issuer-level summary statistics

Issuer variables		Full sample, 1980-2009				Drexel subsample, 1986-1993				Riegle-Neal Subsample, 1990-1997			
		Obs	Mean	Median	St. Dev 4-yr Avg	Obs	Mean	Median	St. Dev 4-yr Avg	Obs	Mean	Median	St. Dev 4-yr Avg
Altman Z-score	Investment grade	6907	2.13	1.75	1.48	2.26	1389	1.83	1.55	1.16	1.92	2109	1.92	1.61	1.27	2.01
	High yield	2652	2.18	1.07	33.59	2.00	456	1.36	1.09	2.01	1.52	807	4.02	1.08	60.79	2.53
	All deals	9559	2.14	1.56	17.74	2.19	1845	1.71	1.43	1.43	1.83	2916	2.50	1.46	32.00	2.15
Cash / book assets	Investment grade	8057	0.04	0.02	0.06	0.05	1736	0.04	0.02	0.05	0.05	2662	0.03	0.02	0.05	0.04
	High yield	3197	0.07	0.03	0.11	0.08	598	0.06	0.02	0.09	0.06	1000	0.06	0.02	0.09	0.07
	All deals	11254	0.05	0.02	0.08	0.06	2334	0.04	0.02	0.06	0.05	3662	0.04	0.02	0.06	0.05
Ebitda / interest Expense (truncated at 0)	Investment grade	7347	13.23	7.72	51.64	21.76	1560	8.91	5.45	24.75	11.60	2430	11.00	6.44	57.48	12.53
	High yield	3002	10.02	3.06	103.90	23.27	557	5.59	2.62	14.37	8.22	956	10.69	2.92	107.93	40.06
	All deals	10349	12.29	6.17	70.89	22.20	2117	8.04	4.88	22.53	10.71	3386	10.92	5.74	75.22	20.27
Leverage (book)	Investment grade	7592	0.30	0.29	0.13	0.29	1610	0.32	0.32	0.12	0.30	2490	0.31	0.31	0.12	0.31
	High yield	2962	0.47	0.45	0.24	0.45	555	0.50	0.47	0.27	0.48	923	0.48	0.45	0.27	0.47
	All deals	10554	0.35	0.32	0.18	0.34	2165	0.36	0.34	0.19	0.35	3413	0.36	0.33	0.19	0.36
Leverage (market)	Investment grade	7519	0.27	0.24	0.16	0.27	1597	0.33	0.32	0.16	0.32	2450	0.29	0.28	0.16	0.31
	High yield	2839	0.43	0.43	0.22	0.42	510	0.47	0.47	0.21	0.46	857	0.44	0.43	0.21	0.42
	All deals	10358	0.31	0.28	0.19	0.31	2107	0.36	0.34	0.19	0.35	3307	0.33	0.31	0.18	0.34
PPE / Book assets	Investment grade	8088	0.41	0.37	0.23	0.42	1741	0.46	0.41	0.25	0.47	2681	0.44	0.40	0.23	0.45
	High yield	3167	0.41	0.37	0.26	0.41	595	0.41	0.37	0.23	0.42	993	0.44	0.41	0.25	0.43
	All deals	11255	0.41	0.37	0.24	0.41	2336	0.45	0.40	0.24	0.46	3674	0.44	0.41	0.23	0.44
Asset market/book	Investment grade	7916	1.79	1.50	0.92	1.80	1714	1.50	1.30	0.64	1.46	2604	1.64	1.45	0.72	1.61
	High yield	3050	1.56	1.31	1.00	1.58	544	1.48	1.26	1.17	1.44	930	1.56	1.31	0.90	1.59
	All deals	10966	1.72	1.44	0.95	1.74	2258	1.49	1.29	0.80	1.46	3534	1.62	1.41	0.77	1.60
Revenues / assets	Investment grade	8110	0.27	0.24	0.18	0.29	1743	0.28	0.25	0.17	0.30	2686	0.28	0.25	0.17	0.29
	High yield	3200	0.27	0.22	0.28	0.29	599	0.35	0.26	0.46	0.37	1003	0.30	0.23	0.38	0.32
	All deals	11310	0.27	0.24	0.21	0.29	2342	0.30	0.25	0.28	0.32	3689	0.28	0.25	0.25	0.30
Return on equity	Investment grade	7912	0.05	0.04	0.31	0.05	1716	0.03	0.03	0.05	0.04	2623	0.04	0.04	0.05	0.04
	All deals	2836	-0.02	0.02	0.34	-0.04	2228	0.02	0.03	0.22	0.03	3488	0.02	0.03	0.16	0.04

44

Tabel 4: New issue summary statistics (continued from previous page)

Panel B: Issue-level summary statistics

Issue level variables		Full sample, 1980-2009				Drexel subsample, 1986-1993				Riegle-Neal Subsample, 1990-1997			
		Obs	Mean	Median	St. Dev	Obs	Mean	Median	St. Dev	Obs	Mean	Median	St. Dev
Principal / assets	Investment grade	8110	0.04	0.02	0.05	1743	0.03	0.02	0.04	2686	0.03	0.02	0.05
	High yield	3201	0.37	0.17	1.64	599	0.49	0.17	3.47	1003	0.52	0.19	2.78
	All deals	11311	0.13	0.04	0.89	2342	0.15	0.03	1.76	3689	0.17	0.03	1.46
Principal	Investment grade	8120	305.96	200.00	395.59	1752	168.60	150.00	133.28	2687	156.96	125.00	154.05
	High yield	3237	232.08	165.00	232.13	609	150.05	105.00	143.98	1010	171.64	130.00	149.94
	All deals	11357	284.90	200.00	358.26	2361	163.81	125.00	136.33	3697	160.97	125.00	153.06
Yield spread (bps)	Investment grade	7374	133.71	108.00	99.16	1571	107.16	95.00	53.54	2122	85.61	77.00	44.30
	High yield	2680	424.30	403.00	178.34	474	433.01	426.00	131.30	612	369.18	354.00	152.67
	All deals	10054	211.17	143.00	179.44	2045	182.69	118.00	158.45	2734	149.09	90.00	143.91
Shelf registered	Investment grade	8120	0.83	1.00	0.38	1752	0.78	1.00	0.41	2687	0.85	1.00	0.35
	High yield	3237	0.17	0.00	0.37	609	0.16	0.00	0.37	1010	0.16	0.00	0.37
	All deals	11357	0.64	1.00	0.48	2361	0.62	1.00	0.49	3697	0.66	1.00	0.47
Callable (indicator)	Investment grade	8120	0.36	0.00	0.48	1752	0.00	0.00	0.06	2687	0.08	0.00	0.26
	High yield	3223	0.13	0.00	0.34	609	0.01	0.00	0.12	996	0.01	0.00	0.10
	All deals	11343	0.30	0.00	0.46	2361	0.01	0.00	0.08	3683	0.06	0.00	0.23
Maturity (log)	Investment grade	6576	2.04	2.30	0.78	1488	2.22	2.30	0.78	2030	1.95	2.30	0.99
	High yield	3139	2.22	2.30	0.31	569	2.25	2.30	0.38	943	2.21	2.30	0.32
	All deals	9715	2.10	2.30	0.67	2057	2.22	2.30	0.69	2973	2.03	2.30	0.85
Subordinated (indicator)	Investment grade	8120	0.01	0.00	0.08	1752	0.02	0.00	0.14	2687	0.01	0.00	0.07
	High yield	3237	0.42	0.00	0.49	609	0.53	1.00	0.50	1010	0.37	0.00	0.48
	All deals	11357	0.12	0.00	0.33	2361	0.15	0.00	0.36	3697	0.10	0.00	0.31
Syndicated (indicator)	Investment grade	8120	0.70	1.00	0.46	1752	0.73	1.00	0.44	2687	0.61	1.00	0.49
	High yield	3237	0.47	0.00	0.50	609	0.41	0.00	0.49	1010	0.43	0.00	0.50
	All deals	11357	0.64	1.00	0.48	2361	0.65	1.00	0.48	3697	0.56	1.00	0.50
Rule 144 A (indicator)	Investment grade	8120	0.07	0.00	0.26	1752	0.01	0.00	0.08	2687	0.02	0.00	0.15
	High yield	3237	0.54	1.00	0.50	609	0.17	0.00	0.38	1010	0.47	0.00	0.50
	All deals	11357	0.20	0.00	0.40	2361	0.05	0.00	0.21	3697	0.14	0.00	0.35
Number of issuers	Investment grade	751				340				418			
	High yield	1225				276				497			
	All deals	1787				584				866			
Number of issues	Investment grade	3237				1752				2687			
	High yield	8120				609				1010			
	All deals	11357				2361				3697			

45

Table 5: The Riegle-Neal Act and ratings informativeness, young issuers

This table reports results from estimating Equation (17) for a sample of public high-yield issuances during a 4-year period surrounding the 1994 adoption of the Riegle-Neal Act in 1994. The main coefficient of interest is the (boxed) coefficient on the interaction of the rating, indicator variable for a young issuer (first public issue $\leq$ 5 years prior to current issue date), and indicator for the period following adoption of the Riegle-Neal act (RN). Models (2) and (4) include age-year interactions. Models (1) and (2) including issues by the same issuer on the same day as different observations, while (3) and (4) combine issues by the same issuer on the same day. Models are estimated using pooled OLS with industry and year fixed effects. Standard errors (reported in parentheses) are robust to clustering at the Fama French 12-industry level; *, **, and *** represent 10%, 5% and 1% significance.

	(1)		(2)		(3)		(4)	
Dependent variable: Log(yield spread)								
Aggregate deals by issuer day	No		No		Yes		Yes	
Age * year controls	No		Yes		No		Yes	
Rating * I(Year>1994) * I(Age<5)	-0.043	***	-0.038	***	-0.032	***	-0.027	**
	(0.014)		(0.014)		(0.013)		(0.012)	
Rating * I(Year>1994)	0.011		0.011		0.009		0.009	
	(0.009)		(0.009)		(0.007)		(0.007)	
Rating * I(Age<5)	0.001		-0.008		-0.003		-0.011	
	(0.009)		(0.009)		(0.008)		(0.009)	
Rating	-0.142	***	-0.141	***	-0.159	***	-0.157	***
	(0.030)		(0.029)		(0.026)		(0.026)	
I(Age<5)	-0.073		0.046		-0.004		0.111	
	(0.152)		(0.160)		(0.148)		(0.153)	
Log(deal principal / assets)	0.075	***	0.075	***	0.067	***	0.066	***
	(0.022)		(0.021)		(0.018)		(0.018)	
Log(book assets)	0.022		0.021		-0.005		-0.007	
	(0.024)		(0.023)		(0.020)		(0.019)	
Has prior rating	0.167		0.174		-0.095		-0.090	
	(0.596)		(0.594)		(0.479)		(0.469)	
Has prior rating * prior rating	-0.021		-0.021		-0.002		-0.003	
	(0.035)		(0.035)		(0.028)		(0.027)	
Syndicated deal indicator	0.018		0.018		0.056	*	0.054	
	(0.028)		(0.027)		(0.034)		(0.034)	
Subordination indicator	0.018		0.016		0.006		0.003	
	(0.046)		(0.046)		(0.050)		(0.048)	
Book leverage	0.025		0.015		-0.030		-0.050	
	(0.136)		(0.140)		(0.171)		(0.176)	
Book long-term leverage	-0.008		0.006		0.003		0.034	
	(0.198)		(0.195)		(0.219)		(0.216)	
Ebitda / interest (truncated at 0)	0.000	***	0.000	***	0.000	***	0.000	***
	(0.000)		(0.000)		(0.000)		(0.000)	
Altman Z-score	-0.054	***	-0.054	***	-0.057	**	-0.057	**
	(0.019)		(0.019)		(0.025)		(0.025)	
Return on equity	-0.066		-0.064		-0.067		-0.063	
	(0.081)		(0.083)		(0.051)		(0.050)	
Property, plant and equipment / Assets	0.293	***	0.292	***	0.266	***	0.265	***
	(0.039)		(0.039)		(0.050)		(0.050)	
Revenue / Assets	0.160	***	0.157	***	0.110		0.105	
	(0.062)		(0.059)		(0.084)		(0.084)	
Market equity / Book equity	0.000		0.000		0.000	**	0.000	**
	(0.000)		(0.000)		(0.000)		(0.000)	
Intercept	7.355	***	7.356	***	7.792	***	7.799	***
	(0.589)		(0.588)		(0.506)		(0.502)	
Number of observations	1866		1866		1278		1278	
R-squared	0.802		0.803		0.822		0.823	

Table 6: The Riegle-Neal Act and ratings informativeness, middle-aged issuers
This table reports results from estimating Equation (17) for a sample of public high-yield issuances during a 4-year period surrounding the 1994 adoption of the Riegle-Neal Act. This table analyzes the impact of the Riegle-Neal Act on issuers whose first public issue was between 10 and 15 years before the current issue. Because the shock to the supply of private vs. public capital was likely less severe for older issuers, I expect estimates of the (boxed) coefficient on the rating, post-RN indicator, and age variable to be insignificant. Models (2) and (4) include age-year interactions. Models (1) and (2) including issues by the same issuer on the same day as different observations, while (3) and (4) combine issues by the same issuer on the same day. Models are estimated using pooled OLS with industry and year fixed effects. Standard errors (reported in parentheses) are robust to clustering at the Fama-French 12-industry level; *, **, and *** represent 10%, 5% and 1% significance.

	(1)		(2)		(3)		(4)	
Dependent variable Log(yield spread)								
Aggregate deals by issuer day	No		No		Yes		Yes	
Age * year controls	No		Yes		No		Yes	
Rating * I(Year>1994) * I(10<(Age<15)	-0.017		-0.021		-0.008		-0.013	
	(0.019)		(0.021)		(0.015)		(0.016)	
Rating * I(Year>1994)	0.003		0.007		-0.001		0.003	
	(0.008)		(0.010)		(0.005)		(0.007)	
Rating * I(10<Age<15)	-0.003		-0.001		-0.001		0.002	
	(0.015)		(0.015)		(0.011)		(0.011)	
Rating	-0.139	***	-0.140	***	-0.158	***	-0.159	***
	(0.031)		(0.032)		(0.028)		(0.028)	
I(10<Age<15)	0.196		0.147		0.115		0.054	
	(0.306)		(0.313)		(0.237)		(0.252)	
Log(deal principal / assets)	0.077	***	0.076	***	0.064	***	0.064	***
	(0.020)		(0.019)		(0.019)		(0.018)	
Log(book assets)	0.020		0.019		-0.006		-0.008	
	(0.021)		(0.020)		(0.019)		(0.019)	
Has prior rating	0.117		0.121		-0.141		-0.142	
	(0.596)		(0.600)		(0.479)		(0.471)	
Has prior rating * prior rating	-0.019		-0.019		-0.001		-0.001	
	(0.036)		(0.036)		(0.028)		(0.028)	
Syndicated deal indicator	0.007		0.009		0.051		0.049	
	(0.025)		(0.025)		(0.033)		(0.033)	
Subordination indicator	0.038		0.038		0.021		0.018	
	(0.052)		(0.056)		(0.054)		(0.055)	
Book leverage	0.046		0.045		-0.006		-0.024	
	(0.174)		(0.176)		(0.196)		(0.196)	
Book long-term leverage	-0.019		-0.010		-0.014		0.016	
	(0.210)		(0.217)		(0.220)		(0.222)	
Ebitda / interest (truncated at 0)	0.000	***	0.000	***	0.000	***	0.000	***
	(0.000)		(0.000)		(0.000)		(0.000)	
Altman Z-score	-0.055	***	-0.054	***	-0.059	***	-0.058	**
	(0.019)		(0.020)		(0.025)		(0.026)	
Return on equity	-0.073		-0.067		-0.074		-0.069	
	(0.078)		(0.082)		(0.052)		(0.052)	
Property, plant and equipment / Assets	0.303	***	0.302	***	0.272	***	0.271	***
	(0.041)		(0.039)		(0.053)		(0.052)	
Revenue / Assets	0.139	**	0.145	***	0.095		0.094	
	(0.060)		(0.054)		(0.083)		(0.081)	
Market equity / Book equity	0.000	**	0.000		0.000	**	0.000	**
	(0.000)		(0.000)		(0.000)		(0.000)	
Intercept	7.523	***	7.466	***	8.014	***	7.972	***
	(0.547)		(0.547)		(0.470)		(0.488)	
Number of observations	1866		1866		1278		1278	
R-squared	0.802		0.803		0.821		0.822	

Table 7: Drexel collapse and ratings informativeness, high-yield issues

This table reports results from estimating Equation (18) for a sample of public high-yield issuances during a 4-year period surrounding the collapse of Drexel in 1989. The primary coefficient of interest is the coefficient on the interaction between the rating and an indicator variable set to 1 during the post-collapse period (1990-1993). This variable is negative and significant in all specifications, which suggests that ratings became more informative after the Drexel collapse for high-yield issuers. Models (1) and (3) use the log of the yield spread at issuance as the dependent variable, Models (2) and (4) use the level. Models (1) and (2) present results for all issues, including those by the same issuer on the same day as different observations. Models (3) and (4) combine issues by the same issuer on the same day. Each model is estimated using pooled OLS with industry and year fixed effects. Standard errors (reported in parentheses) are robust to clustering at the Fama French 12-industry level; *, **, and *** represent 10%, 5% and 1% significance.

	(1)		(2)		(3)		(4)	
Sample: new high yield issues								
Dependent variable: Yield spread	Log		Level (bp)		Log		Level (bp)	
Aggregate deals by issuer day	No		No		Yes		Yes	
Rating * I(Y>1989)	-0.067	***	-20.877	**	-0.078	***	-24.796	**
	(0.022)		(9.246)		(0.029)		(11.615)	
Rating	-0.104	***	-41.617	***	-0.103	***	-40.085	***
	(0.018)		(6.153)		(0.031)		(10.780)	
Has prior rating	1.117	***	464.579	***	0.697	**	315.610	***
	(0.294)		(116.351)		(0.307)		(102.347)	
Has prior rating * prior rating	-0.076	***	-31.468	***	-0.046	**	-20.810	***
	(0.021)		(8.402)		(0.022)		(7.552)	
Log(deal principal / assets)	0.121	***	47.031	***	0.062	*	26.859	**
	(0.044)		(15.958)		(0.036)		(12.784)	
Log(book assets)	0.071	**	30.522	**	0.014		7.940	
	(0.036)		(14.286)		(0.025)		(9.529)	
Shelf registration indicator	0.141	**	60.245	***	0.075		36.416	
	(0.063)		(25.797)		(0.077)		(29.589)	
Syndicated deal indicator	0.028		15.846		0.037		15.533	
	(0.041)		(19.583)		(0.033)		(13.420)	
Subordination indicator	-0.190	***	-77.807	***	-0.164	***	-65.987	***
	(0.050)		(20.615)		(0.053)		(21.369)	
Book leverage	0.197		160.729		0.122		130.799	
	(0.460)		(191.609)		(0.338)		(145.150)	
Book long-term leverage	-0.430		-226.498		-0.447		-234.621	*
	(0.454)		(190.053)		(0.305)		(135.877)	
Ebitda / interest (truncated at 0)	-0.003		-2.381		0.000		-0.855	
	(0.005)		(2.003)		(0.004)		(1.255)	
Altman Z-score	-0.021		1.105		-0.048		-11.119	
	(0.064)		(24.122)		(0.059)		(24.044)	
Return on equity	-0.262	***	-117.117	***	-0.288	**	-133.867	***
	(0.111)		(49.781)		(0.133)		(43.318)	
Property, plant and equipment / Assets	0.116		65.633	*	0.090		56.371	
	(0.081)		(34.386)		(0.093)		(35.443)	
Revenue / Assets	-0.120		-1.241		-0.199	*	-29.953	
	(0.118)		(52.037)		(0.115)		(45.521)	
Market equity / Book equity	-0.005	**	-2.244	*	-0.002		-1.271	
	(0.003)		(1.352)		(0.003)		(1.280)	
Intercept	8.167	***	1142.180	***	8.656	***	1318.112	***
	0.3436		135.1359		0.2706		102.8851	
Number of observations	226		226		158		160	
R-squared	0.741		0.711		0.723		0.701	

48

Table 8: Drexel collapse and ratings informativeness, investment-grade issues

This table reports results from estimating Equation (18) for a sample of public investment-grade issuances during a 4-year period surrounding the collapse of Drexel in 1989. The primary coefficient of interest is the coefficient on the interaction between the rating and an indicator variable set to 1 during the post-collapse period (1990-1993). This variable is insignificant in all specifications, which suggests that ratings informativeness did not change after the Drexel collapse for investment-grade issuers. Models (1) and (3) use the log of the yield spread at issuance as the dependent variable, Models (2) and (4) use the level. Models (1) and (2) present results for all issues, including those by the same issuer on the same day as different observations. Models (3) and (4) combine issues by the same issuer on the same day. Each model is estimated using pooled OLS with industry and year fixed effects. Standard errors (reported in parentheses) are robust to clustering at the Fama-French 12-industry level; *, **, and *** represent 10%, 5% and 1% significance.

Sample: new investment grade issues Dependent variable: Yield spread Aggregate deals by issuer day	(1) Log No		(2) Level (bp) No		(3) Log Yes		(4) Level (bp) Yes	
Rating * I(Y>1989)	-0.020		-1.822		-0.016		-1.515	
	(0.015)		(2.232)		(0.013)		(1.246)	
Rating	-0.120	***	-11.709	***	-0.132	***	-14.011	***
	(0.039)		(4.395)		(0.037)		(3.360)	
Has prior rating	0.104		30.968		-0.135		-38.536	
	(0.830)		(112.258)		(0.651)		(71.811)	
Has prior rating * prior rating	-0.004		-1.352		0.007		1.878	
	(0.039)		(5.212)		(0.030)		(3.263)	
Log(deal principal / assets)	0.085	**	10.215	*	0.066	***	8.389	***
	(0.041)		(5.273)		(0.027)		(3.349)	
Log(book assets)	0.052	*	10.420	***	0.013		5.528	***
	(0.027)		(3.808)		(0.021)		(1.914)	
Shelf registration indicator	-0.103		-15.823		-0.041		-7.756	
	(0.079)		(11.791)		(0.047)		(5.831)	
Syndicated deal indicator	0.044		-3.887		0.084		0.664	
	(0.062)		(7.320)		(0.065)		(6.953)	
Subordination indicator	-0.082		-13.864		-0.011		-5.745	
	(0.052)		(10.032)		(0.038)		(8.064)	
Book leverage	0.363	*	63.020	**	0.291	***	51.955	***
	(0.213)		(28.458)		(0.123)		(9.893)	
Book long-term leverage	-0.235		-47.861		-0.282		-53.106	***
	(0.271)		(32.336)		(0.226)		(19.199)	
Ebitda / interest (truncated at 0)	0.001	*	0.038		0.001	***	0.072	***
	(0.000)		(0.034)		(0.000)		(0.031)	
Altman Z-score	-0.039		-1.405		-0.051	**	-3.856	
	(0.029)		(2.480)		(0.026)		(2.758)	
Return on equity	-0.552		-71.963		-0.289		-31.994	
	(0.346)		(46.371)		(0.203)		(26.485)	
Property, plant and equipment / Assets	0.351	***	39.206	***	0.309	***	33.726	***
	(0.086)		(13.874)		(0.088)		(10.070)	
Revenue / Assets	0.319	**	37.622		0.140		21.502	
	(0.154)		(24.122)		(0.134)		(19.255)	
Market equity / Book equity	-0.024	***	-2.303		-0.024	***	-1.603	
	(0.010)		(1.413)		(0.010)		(1.056)	
Intercept	7.182	***	325.892	***	7.566	***	394.741	***
	(0.703)		(85.654)		(0.664)		(68.491)	
Number of observations	1099		1099		862		862	
R-squared	0.643		0.529		0.655		0.545	

Table 9: Robustness of Riegle-Neal results to window length and event year

Panel A of this table reports results from analysis of the robustness of results relating to nationwide passage of the Riegle-Neal Act in 1994 to the choice of analysis period. The boxed coefficient of interest is the interaction of the rating and an indicator variable for the post-collapse period, and is analogous to the boxed coefficient in Table 5. Panel B analyzes counter-factual choices for the year of Drexel's collapse, re-estimating results from Table 5 using several different choices for the event year. Standard errors (reported in parentheses) are robust to clustering at the Fama French 12-industry level; *, **, and *** represent 10%, 5% and 1% significance.

Panel A: Alternate windows around Riegle-Neal passage year (1994)

	(1)		(2)		(3)		(4)	
Window around 1994	+/- 2 years		+/- 3 years		+/- 4 years		+/- 6 years	
Dependent variable: Yield spread	Log		Log		Log		Log	
Rating * I(Year>1994) * I(Age<5)	-0.054	***	-0.042	***	-0.038	***	-0.023	*
	(0.020)		(0.016)		(0.014)		(0.014)	
Rating * I(Year>1994)	0.012		0.000		0.011		0.016	**
	(0.012)		(0.011)		(0.009)		(0.007)	
Rating * I(Age<5)	-0.016	***	-0.009		-0.008		-0.007	
	(0.005)		(0.008)		(0.009)		(0.013)	
Rating	-0.138	***	-0.136	***	-0.141	***	-0.126	***
	(0.039)		(0.034)		(0.029)		(0.029)	
I(Age<5)	0.160		0.048		0.046		0.149	
	(0.103)		(0.146)		(0.160)		(0.229)	
Number of observations	949		1358		1866		3092	

Panel B: Tests of alternative years

	(1)		(2)		(3)		(4)	
Alternative year	1991		1992		1993		1995	
Dependent variable: Yield spread	Log		Log		Log		Log	
Rating*I(Year>Test year)*I(Age<5)	0.002		-0.026		-0.057	***	-0.014	
	(0.018)		(0.019)		(0.019)		(0.018)	
Rating * I(Year > Test year)	-0.041	***	-0.025	***	-0.003		0.026	***
	(0.009)		(0.010)		(0.010)		(0.009)	
Rating * I(Age<5)	-0.024	**	-0.015		0.007		-0.021	
	(0.012)		(0.017)		(0.017)		(0.016)	
Rating	-0.133	***	-0.121	***	-0.132	***	-0.137	***
	(0.020)		(0.024)		(0.023)		(0.017)	
I(Age<5)	0.555	**	0.342		-0.206		0.349	
	(0.259)		(0.288)		(0.316)		(0.265)	
Number of observations	1265		1362		1517		2448	

50

Table 10: Robustness of Drexel results to window length and event year

Panel A of this table reports results from analysis of the robustness of results relating to the Drexel collapse in 1989 to the choice of analysis period. The boxed coefficient of interest is the interaction of the rating and an indicator variable for the post-collapse period, and is analogous to the boxed coefficient in Table 7. Panel B analyzes counter-factual choices for the year of Drexel's collapse, re-estimating results from Table 7 using several different choices for the event year. Standard errors (reported in parentheses) are robust to clustering at the Fama-French 12-industry level; *, **, and *** represent 10%, 5% and 1% significance.

Panel A: Alternate windows around year of Drexel collapse (1989)

	(1)		(2)		(3)		(4)	
Window around 1989	+/- 2 years		+/- 3 years		+/- 4 years		+/- 5 years	
Sample	High yield		High yield		High yield		High yield	
Dependent variable: Yield spread	Level (bp)		Level (bp)		Level (bp)		Level (bp)	
Rating * I(Y>1989)	-63.656	***	-19.930	***	-20.031	**	-13.848	
	(8.169)		(7.896)		(10.047)		(12.085)	
Rating	11.458		-44.728	***	-36.359	***	-41.689	***
	(18.887)		(7.882)		(5.291)		(7.925)	
Has prior rating	1054.753	***	437.317	***	469.756	***	306.767	***
	(345.503)		(120.098)		(123.847)		(60.710)	
Has prior rating * prior rating	-66.250	***	-30.634	***	-32.179	***	-20.895	***
	(22.861)		(6.444)		(8.581)		(4.215)	
Number of observations	41		121		240		326	

Panel B: Tests of alternative years

	(1)		(2)		(3)		(4)	
Alternative year	1986		1987		1988		1989	
Dependent variable: Yield spread	Level (bp)		Level (bp)		Level (bp)		Level (bp)	
Rating * I(Year > Test year)	-11.927		-21.177	**	-7.949		-7.241	
	(11.739)		(10.656)		(10.548)		(10.563)	
Rating	-31.310	***	-38.346	***	-48.453	***	-64.468	***
	7.857		11.308		7.721		9.202	
Has prior rating	372.116	***	336.443	**	358.135	***	103.673	
	155.870		152.567		85.367		127.067	
Has prior rating * prior rating	-24.674	***	-22.874	**	-24.509	***	-7.957	
	10.455		10.325		5.256		8.670	
Number of observations	187		177		215		208	

www.ingramcontent.com/pod-product-compliance
Lightning Source LLC
Chambersburg PA
CBHW081229170526
45165CB00009B/3009